ONE IN HIM

ANSWERING THE "REAL" LORD'S PRAYER

MARK A. BROWN

Published by Victorious You Press™
Charlotte NC, USA

TITLE: ONE IN HIM
First Printed: SEPT 2022
Editor: LYNN BRAXTON
ISBN: 978-1-952756-84-9 (Paperback)

ISBN: 978-1-952756-85-6 (Ebook)

Library of Congress Control Number: 2022916731

Printed in the United States of America

For details email joan@victoriousyoupress.com
or visit us at www.victoriousyoupress.com

Acknowledgements

A s I reflect on all the people and circumstances that positioned me to complete this book, I realize there are too many names to mention. I will, however, attempt to name those that have figured prominently in this journey (some who may be surprised). Without question, I must first thank my God and Father, who knew me before I was known, who not only gave me life and gave it meaning, but also wired me in such a way that enabled this book to be written. I thank my first family, who I love immeasurably–my father and mother, Luther and Ann Brown, who carried out God's plan for my life so lovingly; my siblings, Helen, Sam, Gloria, and the late Johnny, who gave my life context and substance. I thank my family gifted to me by God, who gave me an opportunity to experience love at the next level–my dear wife, Karen, who put up with me getting up at crazy hours to write and loved me through it all; my children, Devin (and Gina), and Lauren, and the three Brown Boys, my grandsons, Miles, Ethan, and Jayson, who put up with a distracted dad and granddad for a few years as I finished this book. I would also like to thank the many friends and colleagues whose relationships impacted me so deeply that I was compelled to write on this topic. To name a few: my New Life Seventh-day Adventist Church family, my Pine Forge Academy family, Jerome and Kelly Leonard, Patrice Tsague and the Nehemiah Project International Ministries family, Pastor Clarence Crawford and the Teach 'Em to Fish family, lifelong friends from Prince George County, VA, and my colleagues from the U.S. Department of Health and Human Services. You all have shaped my worldview by your presence in my life, and to you all, I say thank you. This book is because you were, and I pray that it will encourage others to embrace the value of "we." May God bless you all.

Table of Contents

Introduction

In John 17:21 Jesus emphasizes His desire for unity among all believers, and this book seeks to address this lofty theme of unity. As I delve into the depth and expanse of its component and associated parts, I am immediately challenged by its seemingly unpretentious three-word title – One in Him. From one person to the next, these words could each have connotations that differ so significantly that it makes this discussion complicated right from the start. What does being 'One' really look like? What does being 'in' really mean? Who is 'Him'? Yet, the call to probe the reality of this phrase, which beckons us all towards unity, had to be responded to, primarily because the prevailing social order appears to be trending swiftly away.

There appears to be an uncontrollable force whose kinetic nature is pulling mankind into a vitriolic abyss, affecting people of all facets of society, and it is gaining strength. And unless something is done to change the downward trajectory of this societal dynamic, mankind will experience a breakdown in every facet of life as we know it. However, I believe there is a more powerful counterforce that preexisted this divisive force and remains present in the world today, a force that created and sustains the cosmos. This force comes from above, from the Creator, and overrules this lesser force, which comes from the created. It is this reality that gives me the confidence to embark on the lofty goals of this book, to not only identify and acknowledge the presence of this synergistic greater force, but to also comprehend and appreciate its intended design for mankind. It is my prayer that this journey into unity will lead the reader to prefer and choose it over the formerly discussed trends, leading us all to what God desires—being a people that are one in Him.

This discussion on unity will take place in a spiritual context. The competing forces often summarized as good and evil are recognized in nearly every belief system, and therefore, can be identified with by almost everyone. However, before a meaningful discussion about unity can be held, it would be wonderful if a platform on which there was room for all belief systems to collectively stand was established. It is recognized that there are several belief systems that should be considered. Monotheism, the belief in the existence of one god or in the oneness of God, characterizes the traditions of Judaism, Christianity, and Islam, and elements of this belief system are discernible in numerous other religions. As such, it is distinguished from polytheism, the belief in the existence of many gods, from atheism, the belief that there is no god, and from agnosticism, the belief that the existence or nonexistence of a god or of gods is unknown or unknowable. All these belief systems have at their root a focal point that serves as the fulcrum on which swings their worldview, and an analysis of these fulcrums could possibly identify a platform for meaningful discussion. However, the breadth and width and depth and height, the complexities, and energies inherent in the effort would overwhelm individuals significantly more learned than I. For that reason, I will address the topic of unity from my perspective as a Christian in hope of at least opening a door through which others will enter, with their perspectives, into a broader conversation that leads to a more complete comprehension of the topic of unity. So, from this point forward, Christian references will prevail.

As the reader progresses through and finishes this book, I pray that they will leave with three things:

- The desire to avoid the inclination to separate and divide

- A reassuring knowledge that they are a part of a big, all-inclusive family designed by God

- A good feeling knowing that they are putting a smile on Jesus' face because His prayer is being answered as His prized creation becomes one, just like He and His Father are one. Hallelujah!!!

With that said, let's get started on this amazing journey, and as we go, let's commit to staying together until we arrive at the place where we are "One...In...Him!!!"

I'm So Glad I'm A Part

A famous author once said that a journey begins with one small step, and as I reflect on how my journey into the topic of unity began, I have come to the realization that often, when that first step is taken, the traveler may not even know that a journey has begun. Often, the full meaning, purpose, and destination of the journey may not crystalize until, at some point along the way, they reveal themselves, progressively adding substance and context to the journey as you advance.

I was born into a Christian family, and because of that, everything about me and my life is seen from a Christian perspective. Therefore, it is safe to say that my explanation for this journey from start to finish will be based on the fact that I believe God directed it all the way. It was by His design that I was the last born in a hardworking family who believed that our very existence was ordered by Him. It was by His design that I grew up in the rural South with a father and mother that insisted we be good neighbors to everyone around us—both those that looked like us and returned the favor, and to those that didn't look like us and sometimes did not. My parents also insisted that we all be our best selves, and that we be intentional about honoring God in all that we do. It was this foundation that led me to become someone who had at his core the desire to live in community with others, to be an asset to it, and to make whatever community I was a part of better by my being there. To me, that is what being a Christian is all about.

I have been driven to write on the topic of unity because I have experienced first-hand and personally the good, the bad, and the ugly of community, as well as the beauty of unity and the ugliness of its absence. I have seen my father, who had a fourth-grade education, support our family in the '60s and '70s as a highly-skilled plasterer, working for an Italian-owned construction company whose owner, Mr. Bertozzi, trusted my father with leadership, making him a foreman responsible for the success of large construction jobs and overseeing men of all races. I heard stories of how Mr. Bertozzi saw the drive and intelligence of my father and, as a result, gave him advice, opportunities, and even resources to start business ventures of his own.

My father schooled his children on how he, being a Black man in the South in that era, skillfully navigated overseeing his peers, negotiating and commanding respect from those in positions of power while also maintaining community with his peers of all races. He shared with his family, especially his three boys, all that was involved—his victories, his defeats, the times when his spirit was watered, and the times when there were attempts to crush it, yet he never gave up on his community. I vividly recall that one of his favorite sayings, usually spoken when his resolve to love his neighbor was being severely challenged, was "People are beautiful." It was also spoken with an inflection and expression that showed his determination to love his fellow man regardless of how he was being treated.

Seeing my mother serve as a domestic and work in a sewing factory in my early years, I recall how she maintained such a loving spirit when her employers spoke to her in the traditionally cordial yet demeaning tones and terms of the South. I saw young Caucasian children call her by her first name, which even as a child, I thought was so disrespectful. Yet, I never saw her show any sign of being offended. When she worked in the sewing factory, her work schedule was so demanding that during the week, I, along with my first childhood playmate, Cousin Edna, would stay with our maternal grandparents, Matthew and Marie Graves, and come home on weekends.

Yet, in spite of these realities of life, my parents maintained a sense of love and unity and inclusion, that allowed everyone in our lives, both those that brought us joy and those that caused us pain, to be recognized as members of our community and to be respected, and to also dutifully require that this respect be reciprocated. It was in this environment that the seeds of unity and community were planted and took root.

As I grew and began to have my own life experiences, those seeds continued to germinate and shape my journey forward. It was my father and mother's example that enabled me to maintain a sense of community in my developmental years when they decided to allow me and my brother, Johnny, to be in the first group of Black children to participate in the integration of schools in that area. And when the Caucasian kids would lean over so that I wouldn't touch them as I got on the bus, when there were fights on the playground for those initial few weeks as children of different races negotiated being in the same space for the first time in our lives, as we were reluctantly allowed to play baseball or be in the band until all involved, both them and us, realized that we belonged, it was our having seen our parents remain honorable in the midst of their experiences that enabled us to do the same.

My siblings also watered my seeds by their examples. My oldest sister, Helen, excelled and became the first in my family to graduate from college in the '60s, enduring racial challenges and becoming an educator and world traveler. Sam, my oldest brother, gifted mentally and physically, working hard on the farm, and literally helping our father build our first home with their own hands. He went on to have a successful career in hospital operations management, as a commercial photographer, and is now leading our family enterprise.

My second oldest sister, Gloria, succeeded in spite of marital challenges, being widowed at a young age with three small children, battling addiction, and yet had a rewarding career as a nurse, an administrator, and obtaining multiple advanced degrees.

And my brother, Johnny, the one closest to me in age, while growing up fought with me and for me. He protected me when we integrated schools, had many personal struggles, and lived a life that many thought was not good—struggling with addiction, never really having a career, and moving from one house to another. Yet, when he passed in 2018, and we reviewed his life and the lives that he touched, we all discovered that he was the one whose heart of gold and love for others exemplified what our family really stood for. And even though he died with both legs amputated from diabetes, he forever stands tall in my mind as a family success story, mainly because of the legacy of unity and community that he left behind.

From all this, my personal, professional, and spiritual life converged to create the perfect storm for the development of this book. When my parents decided to send me to Pine Forge Academy, an all-black Seventh-day Adventist boarding academy in Pine Forge, Pennsylvania, for my junior and senior year of high school, I was enveloped by an environment of kids from various parts of the world, and with teachers and administrators that taught me the value of community and gave me life-long relations. In retrospect, I now realize that it was here that the foundation was laid for this book on unity.

At Pine Forge Academy, I was exposed to the most gregarious, Type A kids from New York City to the most laid-back kids from the Virgin Islands and all types in between. There was the typical mix of skilled athletes, high academic achievers, born leaders, musically gifted, and devious troublemakers that are present in the average high school setting. And because I had a fairly winning personality, was an above-average student, was gifted musically as a bass quartet singer and trombone player, and was a tier-two athlete, I had enough going for me to be socially included. However, I was not a star, was not always a first-pick, was not in the in-crowd but was accepted by them, and was left out enough to remember what it felt like. I remember this initially being of great concern in my teenage mind, but in retrospect, I now realize that this was a significant part of my preparation to write this book.

The remainder of my preparatory journey included matriculating to Columbia Union College (CUC), now known as Washington Adventist University, a small Seventh-day Adventist college in Takoma Park, MD, where my concept of community was expanded to include more diverse ethnic, racial, and the ever so tricky conservative versus contemporary Christianity perspectives. Then, primarily because of my lack of focus, I flunked out of CUC, which led to me transferring to a local junior college, Montgomery College, further expanding my concept of community by more formally including those outside of the denominationally structured environment I had experienced for most of my life to that point. Once again, just like in high school, my marginal social potential was recognized, and I was invited to join a fraternity, which I declined because of my yet unrecognized but developing desire to remain inclusive.

I married my college sweetheart, which began our forty-plus-year journey from an apartment to a rented house, to homeownership—first a townhome and then a single-family home. Life's journey has taken us on paths we could not even imagine we would be traveling on, which included having two children, three grandchildren, being subjected to five bouts with cancer, several career changes, and so much more. Each experience expanded our concept of community to include various economic, racial, ethnic, and cultural levels.

Professionally, I also embarked on a thirty-seven-year career in the federal government, which began in college, initially working with a predominantly Asian and Caucasian team in a biochemistry lab, further expanding my concept of community from a socioeconomic and educational level. I graduated from the University of Maryland with a degree in information technology and progressed from being a technician to a programmer, to a systems analyst, to a program manager of a department-level cybersecurity division. This exposed me to the intricacies of the IT community, often delineated by such things as hardware, software, civil servant, contractor, technical, or management designations. During this time, I also became more involved in my church and my community, serving as a deacon, elder, first elder (next to the pastor in responsibility), and leading and engaging in ministries and organizations locally, regionally, nationally, and internationally. And all these experiences, from the back fields of Virginia to the rolling hills of Pine Forge Academy to the tea fields of Nyamira, Kenya, I now have a better understanding of how it all positioned me to write this book.

Throughout this journey, I have personally experienced and observed the nuances of the back and forth between popularity and obscurity, of being accepted and rejected. I have also become comfortable with and identify with those that inhabited both those realities. And because I experienced both the highs of being 'in' and the lows of being 'out,' I have also developed a strong dislike for the randomness and unpredictability of it all, how the inclusion or exclusion of an individual could be so arbitrarily subjective. In retrospect, I have become keenly aware of how a community could be so easily and casually robbed of a potentially valuable component, how a part of the community that could have been deemed vital by the Creator could be so randomly eliminated by other unknowingly dependent parts.

The realization of how all of my life experiences led to this present place, where this book has become a necessity, was then made clear. I now understand why this realization plays such a prominent role in initiating and sustaining this desire to develop unity in my community, to establish connectiveness between those who are inside of and those who are outside of particular groups. Because of the significance of this realization and the need to refer to it repeatedly in this book, I have decided to give it a label. Let's call it "cognitive disunion counteraction" or CDC, heretofore defined as the ability to recognize the presence of two or more groups of people separated by any number of divisive factors and to actively and intentionally seek guidance from the Creator and engage in drawing those groups together in hopes of realizing His original design for community, i.e. ("One In Him.") ✓

Allah

And so, the perfect storm was created, landing me in a place spiritually and mentally that now gives me the footing to write this book. And as I write from my Christian orientation, I do so fully acknowledging that there are other perspectives from which this could be approached. However, because of the very nature of unity and what is required to achieve it, the perspective from which one begins must remain secondary and surrender to the primary focus of unity. Actually, it would be a dream come true if those of other perspectives would seek to achieve this same goal from their vantage point. That would lead to a more comprehensive realization and validation of the premise of this book. ✓   *Allah*

With that said, I return to my Christian perspective by referencing its core source, the Bible. In John 17, we find one of the most comprehensive prayers of the man called Jesus, recognized in the Christian world as the Son of God, while he inhabited our planet. While the prayer given by Jesus to His disciples in Luke 11 is the model prayer, I consider this prayer in John 17 as the true Lord's prayer because it was His personal appeal to His Heavenly Father. In it, He prayed for Himself in verses 1–5, for He was about to enter into the moment for which he was born, the moment for which he had been prepared 'from the foundation of the world,' (1 Peter 1:20). He prayed for the disciples in John 17:6–19 because He was about to leave them with the awesome task of carrying on what He started—telling the then known world the truth about heaven and the Heavenly (Matthew 28:19, 20). Then, He prayed for the body of all believers in John 17:20–26, for you and me, for the 'whosoever's' of John 3:16 telling us how we could be one in Him.

This leads to a key question—why this book, why now? My first response comes as a result of my experience over the last few years, which is best described as my having broken through the denominational walls that previously and so significantly defined and characterized my spiritual experience, which to a degree had separated me from other believers. Because of this experience, I have been favored to develop beautiful relationships with those of other denominations and have been able to recognize the beauty of their love for God and their fellow man. Those experiences have added a heightened meaning and depth to the phrase, "I'm so glad I'm a part of the family of God." This has led me to realize an alarming truth – that denominationalism has severely hindered the joy that I believe God intends for ALL His children to find in unity. I knew that there had to be something better, that the division and separation inherent in denominationalism could not have been what God desired, no matter how we spiritualize it.

So, as I embarked on this quest to understand and experience the unity Jesus prayed for in John 17, and as I realized its increasing beauty and richness with each progressive step, and with all that I saw happening around me, in society and among the people of God, (recognizing how the latter could impact the former), I knew the answer to that previously mentioned key question. The time for "cognitive disunion counteraction" or CDC is now. Let's go deeper to understand why more fully.

Why This, Why Now?

There are probably thousands of books that begin by lamenting the crazy state of our present world, and few people would argue that fact. Social unrest, increased crime, political instability, pandemics, climate change, and the list goes on and on. And in the face of all these very pressing issues, there is one topic that I believe is both a root cause of many of our societal ills and a key to their solution. That topic is unity, or the lack thereof. As I pondered and prayed about this truth, about the world in which I lived and that my grandchildren will inherit, and about what could possibly be done to change it, I was drawn to John 17. It is this last section that stood out, particularly verses 20–23, where Jesus prays, "I do not pray for these alone, but also for those who will believe in Me through their word; that they all may be one, as You, Father, *are* in Me, and I in You; that they also may be one in Us, that the world may believe that You sent Me. And the glory which You gave Me I have given them, that they may be one just as We are one: I in them, and You in Me; that they may be made perfect in one, and that the world may know that You have sent Me, and have loved them as You have loved Me."

Warren Wiersbe, the prolific Christian writer of the 'BE' series of books, who formerly pastored the Moody Church in Chicago and directed the 'Back to the Bible' radio ministry, described this prayer as Jesus' "final report" to His Father. He observed in the last section of Jesus' prayer that He prayed it for us today so that we would recognize all that He has done for us and given to us and all that He will do for us when we get to heaven. Wiersbe noted that in this section, we see the spiritual priorities that were in the Savior's heart: the glory of God, the sanctity of God's people, the unity of the church, and the ministry of sharing the gospel with a lost world. I join Wiersbe in noting that we today would be wise to focus on these same priorities, and my hope and prayer is that by us embodying what Jesus prayed for, we will be able to join Jesus in saying to the Father what is found in verse 4 of John 17, "I have glorified You on the earth; I have finished the work which You have given me to do."

But it all depends on our ability to grasp what it means to be one in Him. So, we start the discussion with three simple but critical questions—What does it mean to be one? What does 'in' mean? And Who is 'Him'? If we each were to provide our own answers to these three questions, they would probably differ so significantly that it would seem impossible to have a meaningful discussion. Each of us would probably have variations of what being 'one' means, what it means to be 'in,' and although as Christians, we would probably have the same answer for who 'Him' is, our ideas about 'Him' undoubtedly differ significantly.

So, right from the start, we begin to realize the challenges that are present in this discussion. Yet, I believe that the call to unity, which has relentlessly beckoned to me for the last several years, must be responded to by the people of God, especially now. Why? Primarily because it appears that the prevailing social order is trending drastically and destructively towards division, with our differences overshadowing what we hold in common, even, or I should say especially, among the people of God. ✔

Why is there so much division in the world today? There appears to be an uncontrollable force whose kinetic nature is literally pulling mankind apart, driving us into a vitriolic abyss, and it appears to be gaining strength. And I believe that this downward societal trajectory is an existential threat to mankind and the church as we now know it. But this is not a surprise for us, for the same Jesus that prayed this prayer also foretold that this would be the condition of the world in the last days. In Matthew 24:6–10, Jesus says, "⁶ And you will hear of wars and rumors of wars. See that you are not troubled; for all *these things* must come to pass, but the end is not yet. For nation will rise against nation, and kingdom against kingdom. And there will be famines, pestilences, and earthquakes in various places. All these *are* the beginning of sorrows. Then they will deliver you up to tribulation and kill you, and you will be hated by all nations for My name's sake. And then many will be offended, will betray one another, and will hate one another." And so, it is in these last-day times, under these conditions, that we are called to seek unity as a people.

As was stated earlier, this uncontrollable force whose kinetic nature is pulling mankind apart and is an existential threat to mankind and the church as we now know it, will be a topic of discussion in the early stages of this book. However, before we do, we must acknowledge that there is a more powerful Counterforce that preexisted this divisive force, a Force that rules the cosmos, yea even created it. It is that Force that stepped into our nothingness and proclaimed, "Let there be…" This Force remains present in the world today, and I believe that this Force is making that same proclamation regarding unity… let there be!!!

This more powerful Force is named Jesus, and He is a constant reality, for according to Matthew, His last words to His people were "… and lo, I am with you always, even to the end of the age." So, because He is a constant reality, that makes unity an achievable reality. Therefore, another lofty goal of this book is to not only acknowledge the presence of this more powerful, unifying Force named Jesus but to also determine how we can cooperate with Him and be a facilitator of the unity He prayed for instead of succumbing to and participating in formerly discussed prevailing trends around us. This is what calls us to engage in "cognitive disunion counteraction" or CDC. This, I believe, is what will lead to unity, being one in Him.

I also believe that this quest for unity is of God because He has always wanted a people, a worldwide family, as evidenced by the human experience that has evolved from His creation of the Edenic family, to the seed of Abraham, on to the followers of Jesus. I believe 1 Peter 2:9 beautifully describes what God intended His people to be—"a chosen generation, a royal priesthood, a holy nation, His own special people…who once were not a people but are now the people of God." And the glorious ending for this group is described in Revelation 7:9 as "a great multitude which no one could number, of all nations, tribes, peoples, and tongues, standing before the throne and before the Lamb, clothed with white robes, with palm branches in their hands." Yes, God has always had His people in mind. In Genesis 1, after creating man and woman and the family structure, He proclaimed, "Be fruitful and multiply; fill the earth and subdue it," communicating His desire to have a planet filled with His prized possessions and the object of His affection–mankind–living in harmonious communion and relationship with Him and each other.

Even after man sinned, God promised in Genesis 3:15 to send One that would restore what sin had broken, re-establishing the God/man–man/man connection. That promise was made more tangible in Genesis 12, when God promised to bless all the families of the earth through Abraham, presenting further evidence of God's desire for a familial relationship between Himself and mankind. That promise did come from the lineage of Abraham in the person of Jesus Christ, who espoused and promoted an all-inclusive kingdom of God on earth, described beautifully in Galatians 3:26–28, which states that we are all the children of God by faith in Him, where there is neither Jew nor Greek, bond nor free, male nor female, for we are all one in Him.

I believe that God's desire to have His own special people is open to everyone—those who believe in God, those who don't believe in God, and everyone in between. I also believe that the call to unity includes everyone–believers, non-believers, those who have different names for God, and those that don't know Him by any name—because the Bible tells us in 2 Peter 3:9 that our God is not slow or hesitant regarding His promise to save anyone, but is being patient for our sakes, not wanting <u>anyone</u> to be destroyed or lost, but wants all, everyone, regardless of where they are spiritually, to repent and be saved in His kingdom.

So, as we proceed through this book, it is recognized there may be points made that challenge the non-Christian reader. But I am impressed that because of the all-inclusive mindset of God, as those points are encountered, He, through the guidance of the Holy Spirit, will do something that draws us beyond where conversation usually ends and position us for meaningful conversation with non-Christians. For that reason, I cannot promise that this will be a straight-line, predictable journey. But I can promise that it will be an interesting ride, with every effort made to let the Holy Spirit do the driving.

You may ask if it is even possible to reach those of other belief structures, but as I consider the Biblical experience in Acts 17 of the Jerusalem Council and the call to Macedonia and Paul standing in the midst of the Areopagus addressing those who worshiped at an altar with the inscription, "To the Unknown God," I believe that the unadulterated, pure truth of Jesus Christ is for everyone, and that therefore, the concept of being one in Him is achievable. I believe that when the gospel truth is primary, it makes that which divides us – whatever it is – secondary. And because I am a believer in the one true God, and that the Bible is His Holy Word, and that His Son Jesus Christ, who made all things (John 1:3), is the same One who in John 17 prayed this prayer for unity, then He must have a legitimate blueprint for all mankind to be...one in Him.

Now, having established all these foundational points, I believe there are three key principles that must be followed that are critical to the conversation. When employed, these principles will enable us to include many who we may not currently be in conversation with because of our cultural and theological differences. One principle is that we will initially focus on things that we hold in common and build from there. This is Biblical because Amos 3:3 says, "Can two walk together, unless they are agreed?" So, if we intend to journey together towards unity with those we have differences with, we must first find areas of agreement so that we can at least begin walking together.

This is not only Biblical but critical because it paves the way for the second principle to be possible, that establishing

23

and maintaining a relationship is more important than establishing who is right. Applying this principle is made possible when all involved recognize that our goal is not to establish who is right, but to establish what is right.

These two principles are important because their use pave the way for God's truth to be a unifying force. When God's truth stands as its own entity, it is easier for those who discover it to receive it. It is when those who discover truth attempt to claim it as theirs because they discover it first that truth becomes difficult to receive. Many think that they are united racially, politically, economically, and even denominationally, only to discover that division subtly exists and stubbornly persists. I propose that by employing these two principles we can effectively bridge the gaps that exist between us, no matter how great or small.

This lays the foundation for the third and final principle, which sounds simple but is critical and may challenge us at times to maintain. If we are to move towards answering Jesus' prayer, then this principle simply states that we must decide that separation is not an option. If Jesus has prayed that we be one in Him, then like his idea of marriage (Mark 10:8, 9), like the parts of the body (1 Corinthians 12:12, Ephesians 4:16), like the bricks in a building (Ephesians 2:19–22), separation is not an option. Again, let me repeat these three principles: that we focus on things that we hold in common and build from there, that establishing and maintaining a relationship is more important than establishing who is right, and that separation is not an option.

As stated in the previous chapter, my religious experience over the last few years has greatly changed my perspective, and I knew there had to be something better, that the division and separation that currently exists in society and especially in denominationalism, could not have been what God desired for mankind. And after the August 2017 Unite the Right march in Charlottesville, VA, the Black Lives Matter movement, the 2020 election, the events of January 6, 2021, and the vitriolic atmosphere that has prevailed in our country, it became clear that the goal of unity was becoming a fading possibility. The need for the previously mentioned Counterforce, which is more powerful and able to change societal dynamics, is evident. And since I am not qualified to address all societal ills, I will begin by addressing what I see happening among the people of God in the context of denominationalism.

There are many that arrived at their spiritual identity through in-depth study and soul searching which is what God desires. Acts 2:41–42 tells us how the early church was founded, and in Acts 17:11, the Bereans were commended for searching the scriptures to verify what they were hearing from the apostles was true. But I also believe, as discovered in a conversation with my brother Sam, that for many, their denominational identity came as a result of either the family they were born into or the people they encountered at a point of spiritual need, 'who got to them first,' as Sam put it. But I believe that our spiritual identity should be based on more than that.

When I consider the Biblical account of mankind's journey, all I see is the Creator responding to the broken relationship sin caused with His created, and His repeated efforts to restore it and fulfill His desire to have 'a people'. It was this realization that led me to embrace the concept that God's desire for 'a people' extends beyond racial, ethnic, ideological, or denominational designations. Therefore, it may be more appropriate to see these designations as secondary and not primary, more like a community that we, by birth or by choice, have settled into as we all seek God from our own life experiences. It is this concept that led me to a graphical depiction of this journey to God that I believe we are all on.

This graphic is a representation of the collective journey of all who are seeking God in a denominational context. Each one finds themselves on a particular spoke along with others that are there by whatever means their decision was made (birth, choice, etc.), all on their journey to know, love, and serve God. The key points being made by this graphic are as follows:

❖ The gap between the spokes is widest at the outer edge, meaning that the further we are from the hub, representing God, the further we are from each other.

❖ The closer the spokes get to the hub, the smaller the gap becomes, meaning that as God's people draw closer to Him, the closer they will become.

❖ And lastly, if we continue on our journey towards God, we individually meet at the hub, becoming one with God and one in Him.

This concept yields several realities for the Christian community, the body of Christ. If the body of believers would commit to drawing closer to God with this understanding, there would be no need to focus on which spoke you may be on, what denomination you may be in, or to feel the necessity to convince anyone to leave one spoke, or denomination, and move to another. What would be most important is that we encourage everyone that believes in the one true and wise God to respond to His call, continue to move closer to Him, from whatever denominational perspective they may ascribe to, on whatever path/spoke they may be now journeying, and to become one with Him. And as we move towards Him, what we will find is that there is one truth, one faith, one baptism (Ephesians 4:4–6), and as we move closer to the center, like spokes on a wagon wheel, the closer we get to Him, the closer we get to one another, until we meet at the Hub (that could be another name for God) and become One in Him.

My family came from a Baptist foundation and was led to the Seventh-day Adventist church in the 1960s. We are grateful for the truths that have transformed our lives and given us an amazing experience with God in Christ Jesus. But I believe that the realization of what Jesus prayed for offers an even richer experience for me and all believers and calls us to engage in "cognitive disunion counteraction," or CDC. I encourage us to celebrate all who love the Lord but may currently be on a different spoke and to determine how we will connect with them. We are reminded of Jesus' desire for us in John 17:20–23: "I do not pray for these alone, but also for those who will believe in Me through their word; that they **all** may be one, as You, Father, *are* in Me, and I in You; that they also may be one in Us, that the world may believe that You sent Me. And the glory which You gave Me I have given them, that they may be one just as We are one: I in them, and You in Me; that they may be made perfect in one, and that the world may know that You have sent Me, and have loved them as You have loved Me."

So, you may ask, "If this is Jesus' desire for us, then how did things get so bad?" Good question. Let's begin at the beginning.

The Beginning of Evil

It all began in heaven, and several times in scripture, we find heaven portrayed as a unified conglomeration of praise and worship to God. Daniel 7:9-10 speaks of God on His throne with "a thousand thousands" of angels ministering to Him and ten thousand times ten thousand standing before Him. Revelation 4:1-11 shows coordinated praise to God with elders and living creatures worshipping Him. Yet, according to the Biblical account, in the midst of this environment of dedicated worship to God, dissension developed, and an attack on the unity of heaven erupted.

In scripture, we find the essence of what mindset and actions disrupted the unity of heaven and the ill-fated results. In Ezekiel 28:15, 17, we see the fall of a covering angel named Lucifer. It says, of him, "You were perfect in your ways from the day you were created, till iniquity was found in you." In E.G. White's book, Patriarchs and Prophets, she envisioned that little by little, Lucifer came to indulge the desire for self-exaltation. Isaiah 14:12–15 explained it further. "For you have said in your heart: 'I will ascend into heaven, I will exalt my throne above the stars of God; I will also sit on the mount of the congregation on the farthest sides of the north; I will ascend above the heights of the clouds, I will be like the Most High.'" Though all his glory was from God, this mighty angel came to regard it as pertaining to himself. Not content with his position, though honored above the heavenly hosts, he ventured to covet homage due alone to the Creator. "I will be like the Most High." Revelation 12:7–9 shows us the result. It reads, "⁷And war broke out in heaven: Michael and his angels fought with the dragon; and the dragon and his angels fought, ⁸ but they did not prevail, nor was a place found for [b]them in heaven any longer. ⁹ So the great dragon was cast out, that serpent of old, called the Devil and Satan, who deceives the whole world; he was cast to the earth, and his angels were cast out with him."

By reviewing these scriptures, we observe the nature of the created being that led to rebellion against the Creator and the breaking of the relationship between the Creator and the created. We also gain insight into what caused and still causes the fracture in the God/man relationship, which in turn creates the unity-preventing, divisive nature that harms man's relationship with his fellow man today. We will consider five outcomes of this divisive nature:

❖ A desire to be more, to be greater–Even though he was the covering cherub, Lucifer began to look with envy at the relationship between God and His Son. And when they counseled together to determine the creation of the world and the plan of salvation, Lucifer felt that he should be included. It was his desire to be more, to be greater, that the scripture tells us introduced iniquity in his heart and led him to want to be like the Most High. It was this desire that caused war in heaven and for Lucifer and one-third of the angels to be expelled. It is this same desire that adversely affects man's relationship with God and his fellow man.

Eve's desire to be greater led her to fall for the serpent's offer in Genesis 3:5, the promise that eating the fruit would open her eyes and make her like God. And today, man is still on a quest to be greater, to consider his perspective to be equal to God's and to be considered greater, smarter, and more right than other men. And in the context of this book, a major threat to unity is when one's focus is not on knowing God and His truth but on being considered greater, smarter, and more right than others. I believe there is a need for this characteristic to be removed from the people of God, especially within and between denominations. It is not important for us to determine whether we are more right or better than others, only that God is right!!!

The Holy Spirit led me to understand that instead of this desire to be greater, smarter, and more right based on our own 'truth,' we should have the desire for all believers to know and fall in love with God and His truth—because there is only one truth, which belongs to Him. No denomination or group can claim it.

Here is the key: all who believe in God must recognize Him as the source, owner, and creator of all truth and that all must come to Him to receive His truth. Man's claim to have or own the truth feeds the desire to see oneself as being greater, smarter, and more right than others, which robs God of the glory that is due to Him and Him alone, and places it on ourselves, which is what Lucifer did. Oh, let's take heed to this, for this is the beginning of evil. Now imagine what would happen if the opposite were true. Imagine if all nations and kindreds and tongues and people and denominations humbled themselves before God, came together seeking to know and understand His truth, together moving towards Him (remember the wagon wheel), and as our understanding of Him increases, all are led to fall in love with Him and with each other with each passing day. This would allow us, as God's last day people, to experience the unity Jesus prayed for in John 17.

❖ An increased propensity to question God–Lucifer began to question whether God truly is love, whether God's way was the best way for heaven and the universe which led to the broken relationship between the Creator and the created, and eventually between man and his fellow man. At the core of Lucifer's logic, as noted in Isaiah 14:12–15, was his questioning whether the very structure and order of heaven were appropriate. He thought he should be in charge and be higher than God.

Eve was exposed to this logic in the garden, which led her to question whether the order of Eden was appropriate and whether she should settle for the subservient role as the created. Why not eat the fruit, have her eyes opened, and be like God, knowing good and evil?

H. Spence-Jones, in the book, "Genesis," notes that the serpent was insinuating that God was envious of man's happiness and desired to minimize it as a matter of control and superiority. The serpent also wanted Eve to believe that God was not concerned about preventing man from dying from the fruit on the tree that had been prohibited, but was fearful of the created becoming equal to their Creator.

Then lastly, the serpent wanted Eve to think that to be true, which he knew to be false, pretending to be thoughtful of man's safety, while in reality he was only jealous of the honor God had given to man. [1] This is what happens when the created questions the Creator. That is why we are admonished in Proverbs 3:5–6 to trust in the Lord with ALL our hearts and lean not to our own understanding. That is why Jesus in John 16:13 promises us the aide of the Holy Spirit, who will guide us into all truth. We should not develop our own truth or inappropriately lay claim to God's truth. This will keep us from questioning the love, will, and way

---

[1] Spence-Jones, H. D. M. (Ed.). (1909). _Genesis_ (p. 58). London; New York: Funk & Wagnalls Company.

of the Creator without the divine guidance of the Holy Spirit, prevent us from depending on our own selfish and divisive thoughts and perspectives, and allow us as God's last day people to experience the unity that Jesus prayed for in John 17.

❖ The brooding effect–Allowing the imagination to sour the spirit and contaminate the thoughts and actions began in Heaven and played a significant role in breaking the relationship between the Creator and the created, and still today affects man's relationship with his fellow man. As we review this point, it is important that we all take note of how the souring of our spirits and the contamination of our thoughts affects us. It was this brooding spirit in Lucifer that led him to turn against God, negatively influence the angels, incite a rebellion in heaven, leading to the expulsion of himself and all that sided with him.

Do you see how this brooding spirit can affect us? Proverbs 14:12 says, "There is a way which seems right unto a man, but the end thereof are the ways of death." This brooding spirit is driven by thinking our own thoughts, believing that life as we see it is right, and it leads us to our destruction. It causes hatred and division, and if we are not careful, a desire for our thoughts, our view of life, and our need to be the right can lead us, like Lucifer, to glory in our brightness and exaltation. This will have a similar effect on us as it did on him, creating a brooding spirit toward any other person or group that claims to be more 'right' than us. This spirit makes unity an impossibility. We must again trust in the Lord with all our hearts, lean not to our own understanding, in all our ways acknowledge Him as Lord and Savior, the truth personified, then He will direct our path to the unity He prayed for in John 17.

❖ The presence of an unholy influence–This was instrumental in breaking the relationship between the Creator and the created and affects man's relationship with his fellow man today. When Lucifer's spirit had completely turned against God, he began to spread that spirit to the other angels. It is here that the unimaginable is realized, in which the perfect environment of heaven is altered, and the impact of this influence becomes tangible. Holy angels in a holy place falling subject to the influence of one disgruntled being. This experience undeniably establishes why it is critical that we avoid at all cost harboring thoughts and perspectives that draw us away from God and divides His people, and how destructive one person can be who, in pride and arrogance, spreads that spirit to others. By maintaining our focus on God, we, as His last day people, will be able to experience the unity that Jesus prayed for in John 17.

❖ Rebellion ensues–This is the outcome that indicates the nature of the broken relationship between the Creator and the created and has the most damaging effect on man's relationship with his fellow man. Matthew Henry, in his commentary on Revelation 12:7-10, provides additional details about this war, where he draws parallels between this war and the war being waged on earth between good and evil. The seat of this war is *in heaven*, equivalent to the church, which is *the kingdom of heaven* on earth, under the care of heaven and in the same interest. The parties—*Michael and his angels* on one side, and *the dragon and his angels* on the other: Christ, the great Angel of the covenant, and his faithful followers; and Satan and all his instruments; the same combatants as on earth, where this latter party would be much superior in number and outward strength to the church; but the strength of the church lies in having the Lord Jesus for the captain of their salvation. The success of the battle: *The dragon and his angels fought and prevailed not;* on earth, as it was in heaven, there is a great struggle on both sides, but the victory will fall to Christ and his church, and the dragon and his angels will not only be conquered but cast out, destroyed, obliterated. How the conqueror is celebrated: *Now have come salvation, strength, and the kingdom of our God, and the power of his Christ.*

❖ Now God has shown himself to be a mighty God; now Christ has shown himself to be a strong and mighty Savior; his own arm has brought salvation, and now his kingdom will be greatly enlarged and established for eternity. The salvation and strength of the church are all to be ascribed to the king and head of the church. Therefore, it is important to recognize that the war being waged for the souls of mankind is not a war between man and man, or denomination against denomination, but against good and evil. And it is by following the commands of the Captain of our salvation, who is calling all believers to be one in Him, that we, as God's last day people, will be able to stand as one and experience the unity that Jesus prayed for in John 17.

So, all that we are seeing and experiencing today has taken place before. Everything that is threatening the unity of God's people today, previously took place before in heaven–the desire to be more, to be greater; questioning the love, will, and way of God; having a brooding, dissatisfied spirit; being subject to an unholy influence and exercising that spirit on others; waging war against God and His people. Satan brought all of that from heaven to earth when he was cast down, and now, having been shown what led to his rebellion against God in heaven, we must make sure that we are not participants in his rebellion against God on earth. And how do we make sure of this? We do so by determining if we are exhibiting in our lives any of the traits that Lucifer displayed in heaven.

Now, I know that many of us, as children of God, saved and sanctified and filled with the Holy Ghost, may think that there is no way that we are exhibiting the nature of the enemy. But as the Holy Spirit walked me through this part of the study, I was shown how many who call themselves Christians today are exhibiting that very same Lucifer-like nature that disrupted heaven, and that this is what is disrupting God's church (and please note that when I say God's church, I am not talking about a particular denomination; I'm using the Revelation 14:4 definition of the church, those who follow the Lamb wherever He goes). As we look across the landscape of the Christian world today, we see the same thing, large groups of Christians exhibiting the very same traits that led Lucifer to rebel against God and disrupt heaven.

Every group of believers must guard against this spirit and its characteristics: the desire to be more, to be greater (than others that look different, worship different, or have a different Biblical understanding); questioning the love, will, and way of God (in the lives of those that think or worship differently); having a brooding, dissatisfied spirit (when things are not being done a certain way or if anyone else claims to be more 'right'); exercising an unholy influence on others (encouraging people to dislike or discredit other children of God); waging war against God and His people (by marshaling like-minded people against those that don't agree with a certain belief system). I know that this may be somewhat unsettling, but I propose to you that <u>much of what we are experiencing in the Christian world today looks more like a rebellion than a revival</u>, with God's people not being drawn together by God's truth as it is found in His Word, but are instead drawing battle lines based on their different interpretations of God's

Word, claiming that their way is right, looking more to themselves than looking unto Jesus, the author, and finisher of our faith.

I submit that there is a need for us all to take an honest assessment of ourselves, and in order for that assessment to be done thoroughly and honestly, we must allow the Holy Spirit to reveal to us what is in us. We must enter into a John 16:13 experience and allow the Holy Spirit to guide us into all truth–the truth about God, about His Word, about ourselves, about others, and about the world around us. I love the way Matthew Henry's Commentary describes how the Holy Spirit will guide us into all truth. He compares it to the skillful pilot that guides the ship into the port it is bound for. He also says, that to be led into a truth is more than to barely to know the truth; it is to be intimately and experimentally acquainted with truth; to be virtuously and strongly affected with truth; not only to have the notion of truth in our head, but to relish and savor truth, and to have the power of truth in our heart. It denotes a gradual discovery of truth shining more and more: "He shall lead you by those truths that are plain and easy to those that are more difficult."

Here is how scripture describes it in 1 John 2:27 NIV, "But the anointing which you have received from Him abides in you, and you do not need that anyone teach you; but as the same anointing teaches you concerning all things, and is true, and is not a lie, and just as it has taught you, you will abide in Him." 1 Corinthians 2:10 says, "But God has revealed them to us through His Spirit, for the Spirit searches all things, yes even the deep things of God." This is what we will have access to as we conduct this assessment of ourselves to determine where we stand with God in these last days. And I love how John 16:13 ends. It says that He will show us things to come, things that bring clarity and assurance for what lies ahead. But before the Holy Spirit leads us to look forward, He has led us to look backward at the beginning of evil in heaven, and through this backward look, we have a better sense of what is plaguing us and causing disunity today.

Now we can better understand how we can focus on God and have all believers, regardless of what 'spoke' they are currently on, drawn into oneness with Him and into oneness with one another. So, as we now have this understanding and move toward the solution, let's recognize more fully the impact of this rebellion on planet earth and how it has affected the unity God desires for mankind.

The Original Plan, And What Happened to It

Genesis 1:1 begins by saying, "In the beginning God." It is with these words that the Biblical account of Earth's history commences and introduces the concept of a unified Godhead— Father, Son, and Holy Spirit—a concept that is core to God's original design, and that stretches human comprehension. To have three co-existing beings functioning as one is a level of unity and cooperation that is unmatched in the universe. Genesis 1:1–3 and John 1:1–3 tell us that it was this humanly-difficult-to-comprehend, tripartite version of unity that collaborated in the creation of our planet. And though difficult to comprehend, its essence is specifically inherent in the creation of man, evidenced by the statement found in Genesis 1:26 "Let Us make man in Our image, according to Our likeness." It is from this statement that we can recognize how God intended for mankind to function and ex-

ist, having unity that is modeled by the Godhead and the atmosphere of heaven. It is why on two occasions Jesus Christ, the Son of God, prayed for this kind of unity. In the model prayer Jesus gave the disciples in Matthew 10, He said, "Thy kingdom come, thy will be done, on earth as it is in heaven." Then again, in John 17:21, Jesus prayed that we may be one, just as He and His Father are one.

So, based on the centrality of unity in the creation of man and Jesus' repeated desire for unity on the earth, we can conclude that unity is the desired state for mankind. So, why then is unity so difficult to achieve? At the root of this difficulty is the same source that attacked unity in heaven, discussed in more detail in the previous chapter. It was at the fall of man that Lucifer, now known as Satan, once again caused a disruption by leading God's created beings to question their Creator, the same way he caused the angels to do so, and it led to the development of a spirit of separation in man—separation from God and from one another. I believe that it is this spirit of separation, which is older than our planet, that led mankind to have separation from the triune God and the atmosphere of heaven, and that creates humanity's difficulty in achieving unity. With that premise established, we now move forward to analyze the impact it has inflicted upon mankind. Let's first return to the creation story.

Creation was all about love. From the very beginning, the One who created all things, who has been described as the very embodiment of love in 1 John 4:8, put that love on display when He decided to create a world to house His most prized possession—mankind. And that love was evident in how man was created. According to the Biblical account, while everything else was spoken into existence, God shaped man with His own hands. Then, the Source of all life transferred the life-giving spark of life into this lifeless form with a kiss, breathing into his nostrils the *neshamah,* the breath of life, and this combination of body and breath established man, a living soul. And because man was created in the image and likeness of the triune God, and because God is love, when He breathed into man the breath of life, He breathed into him the essence of His love. In this creative act, God introduced love as a primary force in man's existence, the foundation of the God/man relationship and man's relationship with all creation, and especially with his fellow man. And I submit that it is this primary force called love that mankind must employ in order to retain and preserve the original intentions of the Creator for himself and all creation.

But then came the fall. A review of God's commands to Adam and Eve and their eventual fall in Genesis 2 and 3, and by conducting an analysis of Eve's response to the serpent, we find the root of what, in Eden and in our world today, disrupts God's original plan for man and breaks at the DNA level the God/man–man/man connection. This analysis reveals how Eve's response to the serpent was tainted by her personal version of God's commands and how her God-given love turned inward to herself instead of remaining outward toward the Creator and the created. And it is important to recognize that love turned inward is the primary cause of division in the world and in mankind.

Let us now take a deep dive into Eve's response to the serpent, where we will find how her three deviations from God's original command have affected mankind's relationship with God and with each other from Eden until today. We will then follow this analysis with a review of the impact these deviations have had on the God/man – man/man connection:

1. Eve did not mention the tree by name. God said, "But of the tree of the knowledge of good and evil you shall not eat.' Eve said, 'But of the fruit of the tree which is in the midst of the garden, God has said…" The Seventh Day Adventist (SDA) Bible Commentaries state that by speaking of this tree in general terms of locality, she placed it almost in the same class as the other trees in Eden. This was a symptom of <u>awakening doubt in the absolute justice of God's injunction</u> and signaled to the enemy that there was a space in Eve's heart for him to initiate the seed of doubt towards God's character and motives.

2. Eve added additional parameters to God's command. Genesis 2:17, NKJV, states, God said, "In the day that you eat of it you shall surely die." Eve said, "God has said, 'You shall not eat it, nor shall you touch it.'" By adding that parameter, when she touched the fruit and didn't die immediately, it created room for the serpent

to <u>interject substantially more seeds of doubt</u> about God into Eve's heart and mind.

3. Eve changed the weight of the penalty of disobedience. God said," In the day that you eat of it you shall *surely* die. Eve stated, "God has said, 'You shall not eat it, nor shall you touch it, *lest* you die.'" The SDA Commentaries state that by doing this, Eve <u>diluted the full certainty of the death penalty following a transgression of the command</u> and instead declared that death *might* follow such an act. The certainty of the death penalty did not mean immediate death upon breaking God's command, but that at that time, man would pass from the status of conditional immortality to unconditional mortality. The word 'lest' in the original language implies inner alarm at the thought of playing with something that might prove fatal, concealed under an assumed cynical attitude toward the idea that such a thing could ever really happen. In other words, Eve demonstrated a subtle element of disbelief as to whether God would really do what He said He would do in response to her disobedience. All these effects came from Eve's deviation from the direct commands of God.

Now, let's examine what the impact Eve's deviations from God's commands have had on God's original plan for man, on the God/man—man/man connection, and on the unity God desires to have present in the world. You will recall that Eve's first deviation was that she did not mention the tree by name, but by speaking of this tree in general terms of locality, she placed it almost in the same class with the other trees in Eden, indicating doubt in the absolute justice of God's command. This is indicative of what takes place when man does not call sin by its right name, as clearly presented in the Word of God. It removes the aversion to or distastefulness for sin placed in us by God, spoken of in Genesis 3:15 as enmity or utter hatred for sin, thus making the sinful act an acceptable part of life's landscape, of the same class as other behaviors in life, which introduces doubt in the justice of God's command.

When this is done, as with Eve, it signals to the enemy that there is a space in our hearts for him to introduce the seed of doubt about the character and motives of God and of God's people. We see this portrayed in our society today as mankind soft peddles the acts of sin— aggression, hatred, evil thinking, prejudice–and by not calling it by its right name, makes it an acceptable part of the societal landscape. This is a threat to unity today and is addressed in Colossians 2:8, which says, "Beware lest anyone cheat you through philosophy and empty deceit, according to the tradition of men, according to the basic principles of the world, and not according to Christ."

We must adhere to God's original love-based and love-producing commands by calling sin by its rightful name, recognizing God's hatred towards sin, and consider sin's fruit— things like aggression, hatred, evil thinking, prejudice–as unacceptable. When this is not done, sin's fruit shows up, even in God's people, and the enemy sows seeds of doubt about the character and motives of God and other children of God.

That's why we see people who call themselves Christians with bats and clubs, screaming at each other, and hating other people. And if we are not careful, it can happen to us.

Eve's second deviation was that she added additional parameters to God's command. God said, "In the day that you eat of it you shall surely die." Eve said, "God has said, 'You shall not eat it, nor shall you touch it...'" By adding that parameter, when she touched the fruit and didn't die immediately, it created room for the serpent to interject substantially more seeds of doubt about God into Eve's heart and mind, that maybe God was not trustworthy. This is indicative of what takes place when man adds to or alters God's Word and, by doing so, confuses what God requires and what the ramifications of disobedience are. And when by God's grace they survive and sometimes even thrive in their disobedience, the enemy interjects doubt about whether God is being honest or if they even need to pay attention to what God says. We see this portrayed in our society today as mankind distorts the Word of God, altering what God requires by adding their own version of what God says, and when people engage in various acts with no apparent penalty, they become confused about what is right and what is wrong, and about whether they need to even be concerned about the penalty of their actions.

There are many examples of man distorting the Word of God throughout history. It was done by the Pharisees, by pagan religions, by the state-run Roman Catholic church, and by the many Protestant churches that evolved when men broke away from the Catholic church. The Word of God has been distorted as a means for man to meet their own desires, which has led to the creation of different belief systems and much confusion and division. This is a threat to unity today and is addressed in Amos 2:4, "Thus says the LORD: 'For three transgressions of Judah, and for four, I will not turn away its punishment, because they have despised the law of the LORD, and have not kept His commandments. Their lies lead them astray, lies which their fathers followed." We must give all men the unadulterated 'thus sayeth the Lord' so that they will know what is required, what is displeasing to God, and what the price of disobedience really is.

Eve's third deviation was that she changed the weight of the penalty for disobedience. God said, "In the day that you eat of it you shall _surely_ die." However, Eve said, "God has said, 'You shall not eat it, nor shall you touch it, _lest_ you die.'" She diluted the full certainty of the death penalty following disobedience to God's commands and instead declaring that death _might_ follow such an act. As was said earlier, Eve demonstrated a subtle element of disbelief as to whether God would really do what He said He would do in response to disobedience.

We see this portrayed in our society today with mankind assuming that they can disobey God, and when they don't pay an immediate penalty, they think they have gotten away with it and that God wasn't serious about His warning pertaining to disobedience. This leads mankind to lose his fear of the penalty of sin and to continue abusing and misusing one another and dishonoring God with impunity. We see it in the street, we see it on Capitol Hill, and we see this in the house of God. We lie, misrepresent, and mistreat one another. Then, when we don't suffer immediate consequences, we think we have gotten away with something, taking God's mercy for granted, and thinking that we can keep on doing it. This is a threat to unity today and breaks down the God/man and man/man relationship. It is addressed in Romans 6:23, which states, "For the wages of sin is death, but the gift of God *is* eternal life in Christ Jesus our Lord." We must let everyone know that there is a definite consequence to disobedience, though sometimes not immediate, and therefore sin in all its forms must be avoided, and that a way has been provided for man to have victory over sin and receive their eternal reward.

In his book, "God and World in the Old Testament: A Relational Theology of Creation," Terence Fretheim states that as this God/man relationship breaks down, so do all dependent relations to the rest of creation, and that human sin is thought to have the power to break down all of creation.[1]

Isaiah 24:4–6 says, "The earth mourns and fades away; the world languishes and fades away; the haughty people of the earth languish. The earth is also defiled under its inhabitants because they have transgressed the laws, changed the ordinance, broken the everlasting covenant. Therefore, the curse has devoured the earth, and those who dwell in it are desolate."

---

[1] Mathias Nygaard, "Humanity, Theology of," ed. John D. Barry et al., *The Lexham Bible Dictionary* (Bellingham, WA: Lexham Press, 2016).

Jesus, the Son, then came to earth to confirm with God's words and model with His life God's desire for this restoration and healing. This is why He united the thoughts of Deuteronomy 6:5 and Leviticus 19:18 in His response to the scribes in Matthew 22:37–40, establishing the love for God and love for your neighbor as crucial, saying, "On these two commandments hang all the Law and the Prophets." Ecclesiastes 12:13 says that fearing God and keeping His commandments is "the whole duty of man." According to the Pulpit Commentary, that phrase in Hebrew is literally, "this is every man," which means, "this is every man's duty." For this, man was made and placed in the world; this is his real objective, the chief good which he has to seek, and which alone will secure contentment and happiness.[2]

Therefore, fearing (honoring, worshiping) God and keeping His commandments (summed up by Jesus as loving God and our fellow man) is every man's duty and, in essence, is the Creator's prescription to the entire human family for supreme happiness. We must recognize that there are dire consequences when we alter or distort the Word of God and turn the truth into a lie. I repeat what was said earlier–it's all about love.

So, what does this have to do with unity? Galatians 5:22 says that the other player in the creative process, the Holy Spirit, produces love as one of its fruit, and I have heard it said

---

[2] Spence-Jones, H. D. M. (Ed.). (1909). *Ecclesiastes* (p. 306). London; New York: Funk & Wagnalls Company.

that this fruit of love in turn, produces many offspring, one of which is unity—unity with God and with our fellow man. I propose that it is this offspring of love called unity that will champion the cause of ending the downward, divisive trajectory of our society and be the primary evidence of the restoration of the God/man–man/man connection that God originally intended to be present in the world. It is the God/man–man/man connection that God seeks to restore in mankind, which will make unity a reality.

Jesus spoke repeatedly of the powerful witness unity will have in the world. In John 13:35, He said, "By this all will know that you are My disciples, if you have love for one another." Then, He said it twice in His prayer for all believers, saying that our unity will prove to the world that God has sent Him. I believe that is why God is calling us to recognize the importance of unity at this time in earth's history. And I also believe that it will be done on the earth today because the Holy Spirit will do as it did during creation, hover over our chaos and divisiveness like He hovered over our planet, which at that time, was without form and void and covered in darkness (sounds like our world today). The hovering Holy Spirit is preparing all mankind for the explosively creative work of God that will restore His original design in the hearts of those who will receive Him, removing the fruit of sin and the division and disunity it causes, and create that group known as God's own special people, that will follow the Lamb wherever He goes and will be among that number seen by John rejoicing in heaven.

So, there you have it. We have reviewed the original plan and what happened to it, and how it can and will be restored. And now my prayer is that God's people everywhere will avoid the mistakes made in Eden, that we will trust the character and motives of God, obey Him explicitly and allow Him to repair in us what has been broken, and be moved by love to engage in "cognitive disunion counteraction" (CDC) so that His people on earth can become one and be prepared for our kingdom in heaven.

In the next chapter, we will begin to unpack how broken and divided the church is and lay the groundwork for how God will repair it. In preparation for that exercise, I leave you with the promise found in Philippians 1:6, which says, "Being confident of this very thing, that He which hath begun a good work in you will perform it until the day of Jesus Christ." Hallelujah!!! Thank you, Jesus!!!

Separation Nation

As we look at the Christian landscape today, it's mind-boggling how people who say they serve the same God and who say they use the same Bible as their guidebook are so divided. When we go back to the fall of man, right after Adam and Eve disobeyed God by eating the forbidden fruit and realized that they had been caught in their sin, we immediately see the divisive nature of sin. As shown in Genesis 3:12–13, the first thing they did, in an effort to feel right again, was accuse someone or something else as the reason for doing wrong. Here is where a key element of division was first realized. As we look across the societal and religious landscape today, what we consistently see is one group saying that they are right and the other group is wrong, with some even going as far as saying that the problems of the world exist because of someone else being wrong.

From a societal perspective, this mindset has caused different cultures and races to hold many negative beliefs about others, creating and sustaining an adversarial view toward others. Though not grounded in fact, the necessity for those views to be sustained is fueled by the need for one group to be 'wrong' so that the other group can feel more 'right.' In the Edenic example, we see how far this dynamic can go when Adam seemed to not only blame Eve for his mistake, but he even blamed God for creating the woman that led to his error. In Genesis 3:12, Adam said, "The woman whom <u>You</u> gave to be with me, she gave me of the tree, and I ate." Then in verse 13, the woman said, "The serpent deceived me, and I ate."

Here, at the very inception of sin, we see the guilty parties insinuating that things would be much better if someone else hadn't been wrong. It is this very same sentiment that is plaguing our society today. One group is saying, "Things would be much better if that other group wasn't so wrong or so bad." But in the context of this discussion, our focus is on the occurrence of this dynamic in the religious world. Since the seed of Abraham was designated as God's special people, there has been a desire for those identifying themselves as such to consider themselves as being spiritually superior to others. It is worthy to note that a common perspective of many religions and denominations is that of being God's special people and therefore knowing the will and way of God better than others. This is the root cause of divisions and disunity among believers and gives birth to what I have termed 'separation nation.'

In the introduction of the book, "The Religions Book: Big Ideas Simply Explained," the authors state that there is no simple definition of the concept of religion that fully articulates all its dimensions. Encompassing spiritual, personal, and social elements, this phenomenon is, however, universal, appearing in every culture from creation to the modern days. It has led men to establish their own belief systems, 'bibles' or books that communicate their belief system, ways of living, and reasons for and methods of proselytizing those that don't believe as they do. Yet, in all their efforts to establish their religion as the 'right' religion, all that appears to happen is that the division between us grows wider. It has also led many to be cautious of how information regarding religion is received from others, making us suspicious and less likely to consider the ideas of others, therefore reducing the possibility of coming together in unity.

It is amazing how comfortable and content many have become with being divided. Be it racially, denominationally, generationally, culturally, or ideologically, almost everyone has accepted that the need to be divided is a necessity. When expectations are not met, when references are not catered to, and when fears are realized, we separate from those who we believe are the cause of our discomfort. And what is most dangerous is when division and the reasons for it are so fully accepted that it is believed that there is no longer a need to address it or even discuss it. It is then that more insidious habits set in, when we figure out ways to behave cordially and acceptable and learn to coexist while holding on to these divisive beliefs—and not only do we feel justified but even righteous in our positions. We feel so comfortable with it that we begin to actually believe we can come into the presence of God and seek to serve and represent a God of love and unity, all while a totally contradictory and incompatible divisiveness resides at the core of our very being. We can be saying and doing the spiritually and socially acceptable things that we hope project a loving, kind, and godly spirit while simultaneously, whether consciously or subconsciously, possessing a divisive mindset that is the polar opposite to that of the God we say we represent.

In His Word, God speaks directly to those who try to live for Him and serve Him with a two-track mind, or what is called experiential duality. James 1:5–8 speaks to those that attempt to know and serve God but believe and live in ways that are contrary to God. It says, "If any of you lacks wisdom, let him ask of God, who gives to all liberally and without reproach, and it will be given to him.[6] But let him ask in faith, with no doubting, for he who doubts is like a wave of the sea driven and tossed by the wind.[7] For let not that man suppose that he will receive anything from the Lord;[8] he is a double-minded man, unstable in all his ways."

The Holman New Testament Commentaries says that these verses outline our resources for facing trials and explain how to get through them. Christians need wisdom and faith as they encounter trials. We are encouraged to pray for wisdom and to pray with faith. It was believed at the time of this writing that Jewish Christians should understand wisdom. To James and to Jews, wisdom was much more than knowledge and intelligence. Judaism emphasized that "the fear of the Lord" was the starting point of wisdom (Prov. 1:7). Wisdom was a spiritual trait that developed from a wholehearted love for God's ways.[3] It is this wholehearted love for God's ways that will deliver us from behaving in ways that are contrary to God's ways. It is this same wholehearted love for God's ways that will lead believers to say as David did in Psalm 119:112–114, "[112]I have inclined my heart to perform Your statutes forever, to the very end. [113]I hate the double-minded, but I love Your law. [114]You are my hiding place and my shield; I hope in Your word." It is this wholehearted love for God's ways that will lead us to do as James 4:8 instructs us to do—to "Draw near to God and He will draw near to you. Cleanse *your* hands, *you* sinners; and purify your hearts, you double-minded."

It is important for us to grasp these instructions today because if we remain double-minded, trying to serve a God of love and unity while living a life of hatred and disunity, our spiritual hearts will become numb, and our spiritual eyes will become blind. We won't sense or see the dangerous condition in which we are in, a condition that makes unity virtually impossible. And this condition has one telltale symptom–the absence of love. Members of every denomination must determine if this symptom is present, and it is time for this determination to be made here and now. It is on this point that every believer must do some soul searching, because much of what we see in our society is a direct result of believers being in this dangerous, ungodly, unrighteous, unity-preventing,

---

[3] Lea, T. D. (1999). *Hebrews, James* (Vol. 10, p. 258). Nashville, TN: Broadman & Holman Publishers.

loveless condition. And if the people of God can't get this right, what can we expect from those that don't serve God? In keeping with what is said in 1 Peter 4:17–18, it is time for judgment on the issue to begin in the house of God.

Denominations or groups are generally formed based on a perceived grasp of "the truth," and this perception inherently includes the belief that they alone have or possess or own that truth. This belief of having or owning the truth invariably creates the belief that having "the truth" makes them the 'right' religion or denomination, which therefore leads them to believe that everyone else is 'wrong' and gives them a self-defined righteousness that is not of God and causes division among believers. Having this belief creates an opportunity for the enemy to interject a divisive nature into the body of believers.

At this point, it is important to define believers; after all, it was Jesus' prayer for all believers that started this book. In John 17:20, Jesus said, "I do not pray for these alone, but also for those who will believe in Me through their word." Therefore, it is important that we have a proper concept of the scope of who Jesus was referring to. Believers are those that believe in God the Father, God the Son, God the Holy Spirit, and believe in His Word. They may have differing understandings, but they are all believers. And what must be avoided at all costs are those things that divide believers and prevent us from coexisting as we grow in the knowledge of God and His Word.

All believers must recognize that there is a threat to the unity that God desires us to have, and we must become like the people in Isaiah 64, recognizing how utterly repulsive we all are, admitting as they did in verse 6, "We are all like an unclean thing, and all our righteousnesses are like filthy rags." Please take note of the words, "our righteousnesses." I noticed this phrase and its significance for the first time during this writing. For years, I have quoted this text by saying that "our righteousness is like filthy rags," but that is misquoting the text. It says, "our righteousnesses"—plural, are like filthy rags. The Holy Spirit helped me to understand that the plurality of this phrase is important because it indicates a plague of pandemic proportions among Christian believers, the presence of various strands of the virus among God's people known as "our righteousnesses," which are versions of righteousness of our own making, unholy copies, knock-offs if you will, imitations of God's righteousness that are made of our own ingredients, our own values, and our own ideas.

The righteousness that we must seek is entered into when we as a repentant sinner are justified by faith and is spoken of in Romans 5:1 as having at "peace with God." We must recognize that it was obedience on Christ's part to the righteous requirements of the law that made it possible for Him to justify or to declare 'righteous' those who come to Him by faith, fully resting on His sacrifice and not their own attempts to be righteous. It is with this understanding that we as God's people today must determine whether we are like an unclean thing, infected by this virus that leads us to rest on our own filthy rags-like righteousnesses.

Isaiah 64:6 tells us what happens as a result, "We all fade as a leaf," the light of Christ in us diminishes, and we lose our luster because as a leaf separated from a vine soon withers and dies, so do believers who separate from the vine, Christ Jesus. We fade, the glow of Christ's love grows dim, and we die. The effect of sin is death.[4] This scripture then says, "And our iniquities, like the wind, have taken us away." As the wind tears a leaf from a branch and carries it farther and farther from the parent tree and thus from its source of life, so does this sinful condition, sweep man farther and farther away from God, and hurries him on toward death and destruction.[5] It then opens the door to the evil thoughts and behaviors that now seem to be inherent to the Christian experience today, leading many "Christians" to think horrible thoughts about others, do horrible things to others, dislike others, hate others, mistreat others, even kill others, all while still believing we are righteous because according to our "righteousnesses," we have "the truth," and others do not. This is what Christianity looks like today. This is Separation Nation. Oh, Lord, have mercy on us.

---

[4] Nichol, F. D. (Ed.). (1977). *The Seventh-day Adventist Bible Commentary* (Vol. 4, pp. 327–328). Review and Herald Publishing Association.

[5] Nichol, F. D. (Ed.). (1977). *The Seventh-day Adventist Bible Commentary* (Vol. 4, p. 328). Review and Herald Publishing Association.

For a Biblical example of this, let us conduct a high-level review of the first twelve verses of Matthew 23 and consider the words of Jesus as He presents his observations of the scribes and Pharisees. And as we consider this, let us do an honest assessment – individually, congregationally, and denominationally – to determine whether we resemble what Jesus is warning against, whether we are infected with this dangerous, ungodly, unrighteous, unity-preventing, loveless condition, whether we have separated from the vine, and our love and Christianity is fading, even dying. Here we see Jesus taking this opportunity, with a scathing denunciation against the scribes and Pharisees, to break the chains that bound the people to tradition and to those who perpetrated it. This is the reason why it is important for us to do this assessment so that we, too, can identify and break the chains that bind us to anything that is not of God and to anybody that perpetuates it.

In reading the New Living Translation, notice the warning given in Matthew 23:1–8. The scripture says, [1]"Then Jesus said to the crowds and to His disciples" (notice the audience; Jesus has already spoken three impassioned parables against the scribes and Pharisees and successfully responded to their questions, yet their response to Jesus remains the same as their response to John the Baptist,[6] so He now is speaking words of warning to the people and to His disciples (and to us), [2]"The

---

[6] Mangum, D. (Ed.). (2020). _Lexham Context Commentary: New Testament_ (Mt 23:1–39). Bellingham, WA: Lexham Press.

teachers of religious law and the Pharisees are the official interpreters of the law of Moses.[a] ³ So practice and obey whatever they tell you, but don't follow their example. For they don't practice what they teach." (**Here is a checkpoint**: Do we sit as Biblical and spiritual authorities, yet our example is tainted because we don't practice what we teach or preach)?

⁴ "They crush people with unbearable religious demands and never lift a finger to ease the burden" (**Here's another checkpoint**: are we burdening people with do's and don'ts, or are we burden bearers, showing people how the burden of sin is lifted at Calvary?). ⁵ "Everything they do is for show. On their arms they wear extra wide prayer boxes with Scripture verses inside, and they wear robes with extra-long tassels." (**Another checkpoint**: do we do things for show, big Bibles, well dressed on the outside but wretched and empty on the inside)? ⁶ "And they love to sit at the head table at banquets and in the seats of honor in the synagogues. ⁷ They love to receive respectful greetings as they walk in the marketplaces, and to be called 'Rabbi'" (or elder or evangelist or prophet or doctor, or whatever title it is that makes us feel important).

Now, Matthew 23:8–12 provides steps to take to avoid being like the scribes and Pharisees. ⁸ "Don't let anyone call you 'Rabbi,' for you have only one teacher, and all of you are equal as brothers and sisters."[d] (and as believers) ⁹ "And don't address anyone here on earth as 'Father,' for only God in heaven is your Father. ¹⁰ And don't let anyone call you 'Teacher,' for you have only one teacher, the Messiah. ¹¹ The greatest among you must be a servant. [12] But those who exalt themselves will be humbled, and those who humble themselves will be exalted."

As we see, these last five verses reflect Jesus' efforts to keep His children in the right frame of mind, to remember who they are and on whom they must depend. All believers must recognize that our "righteousnesses" comes as a result of our desire to be called a certain title or be honored a certain way, or by following a certain tradition. Desiring those things and thinking in that way exposes us to that dangerous, ungodly, unrighteous, unity-preventing, loveless condition that we spoke of earlier, that condition that is not of God and keeps us in this Separation Nation mentality.

As I close this chapter, I want to point out one sobering outcome from having this Separation Nation mentality. As we discussed earlier in Matthew 23, Jesus' warning to the people of His day about this mentality and how to avoid it extends to us today. And following this section of scripture, we see that Jesus pronounces seven woes against the scribes and Pharisees. It is the second woe in verse 15 that is quite alarming and must be considered closely by us as God's last day people seeking to spread the gospel of Jesus Christ. It reads, "What sorrow awaits you teachers of religious law and you Pharisees. Hypocrites! For you cross land and sea to make one convert, and then you turn that person into twice the child of hell[a] you yourselves are!"

My Lord, this shook me to the core. I heard an expansion of this text by a speaker at the 1888 Message National Study Conference, a group whose objective was to study and learn more about the message of Righteousness by Faith which was presented by Alonzo T. Jones and Ellet J. Waggoner to the 1888 General Conference session of Seventh-day Adventists. He said that because God's people do not have a proper understanding of the gospel and because they have not surrendered to the Holy Spirit in understanding and living the gospel, they are in a Laodicean state (see Revelation 3:14–22). The speaker then said that this is the cause of God's delay in pouring out the latter rain, which in the Seventh-day Adventist belief represents the outpouring of God's Holy Spirit in the last days that will enable and empower His people to spread the gospel. And while God wants to pour out the latter rain, He cannot pour it out on His people while they are in this state because He does not want this Laodicean mindset to go viral.

Many today are praying and crying out to God for the latter rain so that we can go forward with the power to evangelize and finish this great work of spreading the gospel. Many want the power, but few want to surrender. The speaker wanted us to understand that without full and complete surrender to God, our self-defined "righteousnesses" have made us unfit to receive the latter rain. And if God were to pour out the latter rain on us while we have an improper mindset, then we would spread that mindset around the world, and what was said of the scribes and Pharisees in Matthew 23:15 could be said of us— "What sorrow awaits you teachers of religious law and you Pharisees. Hypocrites! For you cross land and sea to make one convert, and then you turn that person into twice the child of hell[a] you yourselves are!" This is saying that our evangelistic campaigns would create converts that are twice as bad as we ourselves are – twice as ungodly, twice as unrighteous, twice as loveless, twice as divisive. Lord, have mercy!!!

We must recognize that our "righteousnesses" are as filthy rags. Lord, help us to understand this and instead strive to be Christ-like Christians. But we must not worry. God promises to repair what the enemy has broken. He says, in Ezekiel 36:25-27 NKJV, [25] "Then I will sprinkle clean water on you, and you shall be clean; I will cleanse you from all your filthiness and from all your idols. [26] I will give you a new heart and put a new spirit within you; I will take the heart of stone out of your flesh and give you a heart of flesh. [27] I will put My Spirit within you and cause you to walk in My statutes, and you will keep My judgments and do them." The kingdom of God will replace Separation Nation. Let's hang in there. It will be done in Jesus' name!!!

The Pre-Problem Solution

At the end of the previous chapter, we recognized and celebrated the fact that God will fix what has been broken, that He will repair and prepare His own special people for His coming kingdom. Now, it's time for us to rejoice in the fact that God has always had a solution to the sin problem, even before there was a problem. I believe that right now, God is calling out across the world, and people are hearing and responding to that call. And I believe that people are taking different paths to God as they respond to that call, based on their culture, history, and personal experiences, which presently may have them on different spokes of that wagon wheel we spoke about earlier. Because of this, I also believe that what we must do is accept and acknowledge every believer as they respond to the call of God, following the Biblical admonition to look unto Jesus, the author, and finisher of our faith, moving toward Him as their knowledge of <u>His</u> truth (the only truth) grows. And as we all move closer to Him, we will move closer together, reducing with each step the things that divide us until we meet at the Hub, Christ Jesus, and making us one in Him. Hallelujah!!!

In Chapter 1, we discussed how the problem began in heaven when Lucifer allowed iniquity to enter his heart, leading him to want to be like the Most High. It was this infection of iniquity that caused war in heaven and led to Lucifer and one-third of the angels being expelled. But in those very counsels between the Father and the Son, which Lucifer envied, not only were the plans for creating the world developed, but also the plan of salvation, the pre-problem solution. Matthew Henry's Commentary says, "It (the plan of salvation, the pre-problem solution) is prepared *from the foundation of the world*. This happiness was designed for the saints, and they, the saints, all those who would respond to the call of God, were prepared for it, before time began, from all eternity (let's allow that to sink in for a minute).

Ephesians 1:4 says, that He (God) chose us in Him (Jesus) before the foundation of the world and that we should be holy and without blame before Him (God) in love. The end (the resolution of the sin problem and the restoration of man), which is last in execution, is first in intention (also allow this to sink in for a minute). In other words, the solution and its execution were first in God's mind before the problem even existed. Infinite Wisdom always had an eye for the eternal glorification of the saints, from the first founding thoughts of the creation. We must understand that the preparation of the place of this happiness, which is to be the seat and habitation of the blessed, was in place in the very beginning of the work of creation, already a part of 'in the beginning' found in Gen. 1:1. Job 38:4–7 tells us that in the heaven of heavens, the morning stars were singing together when the foundations of the earth were fastened. Why? Because they knew what the glorious, intended ending would be.[7] In Wiersbe's "The Bible Exposition Commentary," it is noted that <u>God chose us even before He created the universe so that our salvation is wholly of His grace and not on the basis of anything we ourselves have done.</u> He chose us *in Christ*, not in ourselves. And He chose us for a purpose: to be holy and without blame.

In the Bible, an election is always *unto* something. It is a privilege that carries a great responsibility. <u>Does the sinner respond to God's grace against his own will? No, he responds because God's grace makes him willing to respond.</u> The mystery of divine sovereignty and human responsibility will never be solved in this life. Both are taught in the Bible. John 6:37 says, "All that the Father gives Me will come to Me, and the one who comes to Me I will by no means cast out." This scripture supports the wagon wheel analogy, confirming that <u>all those that are coming to Jesus, regardless of which spoke they might be on, He will by no means cast out.</u> As it pertains to divine sovereignty and human responsibility, both are true, and both are essential. God has made up His mind, and it shows in His divine sovereignty by the all-encompassing plan of salvation, and when the child of God responds to His call,

---

[7] Henry, M. (1994). *Matthew Henry's commentary on the whole Bible: complete and unabridged in one volume* (p. 1751). Peabody: Hendrickson.

it will show as they take up the human responsibility by choosing Jesus.

You will also note that just as all three Persons of the Godhead were involved in the creation, they are also involved in our salvation. 1 Peter 1:3 proves it by stating, "Blessed be the God and Father of our Lord Jesus Christ, who according to His abundant mercy has begotten us again to a living hope through the resurrection of Jesus Christ from the dead." As far as God the Father is concerned, his children are saved when He chose them in Christ in eternity past. But that alone did not save us. As far as God the Son is concerned, we were saved when He died for us on the cross. And as far as God the Spirit is concerned, we were saved when He moved in our hearts to yield to His conviction and received Christ as your Savior. What began in eternity past is fulfilled in time present and will continue for all eternity![8] So, we see in marvelous ways that God had an incredible solution in place before the problem of division and disunity even existed. Yes, the solution preexisted the problem, and what we see throughout the Bible is God in various ways showing mankind that even though they had fallen into sin, the defining moment for mankind was not the fall but the pre-problem solution. Stated another way, in God's eyes, what defines man is not man's fall but God's preexisting provision for man's salvation. So that we can recognize what is most important as we try to determine who God's children are, let me say that again—what defines man is not man's fall

---

[8] Wiersbe, W. W. (1996). _The Bible exposition commentary_ (Vol. 2, p. 11). Wheaton, IL: Victor Books.

but God's preexisting provision for man's salvation, the pre-problem solution. And it is this pre-problem solution that provides everyone, regardless of race, ethnicity, social status, denomination, or belief system (the spoke that they are presently on), with the privilege of being a child of God.

This is what makes 1 Peter 2 so instructional for us right now as we realize what God has done for us just so we can be one in Him. Let's spend some time reviewing what Peter says, so that we can better understand how God intends for us to live together as believers. 1 Peter 2:1–5 NKJV says, "Therefore, laying aside all malice, all deceit, hypocrisy, envy, and all evil speaking, as newborn babes, desire the pure milk of the word, that you may grow thereby, if indeed you have tasted that the Lord is gracious. Coming to Him as to a living stone, rejected indeed by men, but chosen by God and precious, you also, as living stones, are being built up a spiritual house, a holy priesthood, to offer up spiritual sacrifices acceptable to God through Jesus Christ."

Let's look more closely at the component parts of this instructional section of scripture because, in it, we find the building blocks of what the family of God should look like and how it should operate:

- Laying aside all malice, all deceit, hypocrisy, envy, and all evil speaking – the *Seventh-Day Adventist Bible (SDA) Commentary* says that this laying aside means 'stripping off' as clothing. *Wuest's Word Study* says that Peter singles out five sins that the recipients of this

letter were guilty of and that some of us may struggle
with today. The Greek word translated "malice" refers
to any kind of wickedness. "Guile," or deceit, is the
translation of a word that in its verb form means "to
catch with bait," and in the noun form, which Peter
uses, means "craftiness." The word "hypocrisies" is the
transliteration of the Greek word, which means literally "to judge under," as a person giving off his judgment from behind a screen or mask. The true identity
of the person is covered up. It refers to acts of imper-
sonation or deception. It was used by an actor on the
Greek stage. Taken over into the New Testament, it referred to a person we call a hypocrite, one who assumes the mannerisms, speech, and character of
someone else, thus hiding his true identity. Christianity requires that believers should be open and above-
board. They should be genuine, not fake. Their lives
should be like an open book, easily read. *All envies:*
everything that may be called *envy*, which is a grieving
at the good and welfare of another, at their abilities,
prosperity, fame, or successful labors.[9] The word "evil
speaking" is in the Greek text "speaking down" to a
person, referring to the act of defaming, slandering,
speaking against another.[10]

---

[9] Henry, M. (1994). *Matthew Henry's commentary on the whole Bible: complete and unabridged in one volume* (p. 2425). Peabody: Hendrickson.

[10] Wuest, K. S. (1997). *Wuest's word studies from the Greek New Testament: for the English reader* (Vol. 11, pp. 49–51). Grand Rapids: Eerdmans.

The traits listed here represent those things that must not be found in the Christian. And everyone who calls themselves a Christian must assess whether any of these things exist in them. Do we have any of these feelings toward others – believers, nonbelievers, neighbors, other races, those of a different political party, or even another denomination? We each must do this assessment. Emotions have been running so high lately, even among believers, with Black Lives Matter and Make America Great Again, and whether we should wear masks or get vaccinated, believers everywhere need to check themselves. The fact is that if we have any of these feelings toward <u>anyone</u>, Peter is calling for us to lay them aside and strip them off so that we can be one in Christ Jesus.

- As newborn babes, desire the pure milk of the word, that you may grow thereby–Peter here is not thinking of milk as an infant diet to be replaced by meat. In Peter's example, the milk of the abiding word is simply the Christian's necessary food.[11] The SDA Commentary reminds us that we all must long eagerly for the Word as a newborn baby longs for its mother's milk. Similarly, each Christian should long for the spiritual nurture of the Scriptures, especially the milk of God's Word that provides the simple, elementary, fundamental principles of the gospel. The prerequisite to the

---

[11] Clowney, E. P. (1988). *The message of 1 Peter: the way of the cross* (p. 78). Leicester, England; Downers Grove, IL: InterVarsity Press.

act of intensely yearning for the Word of God is the act of once and for all putting sin out of our lives. <u>Sin in the life destroys the appetite for the Word</u>. The Christian who tries to find satisfaction in the husks of the world, like the prodigal son, has no appetite left for the things of God. The heart filled with the former has no room for the latter. A healthy infant is a hungry infant. A spiritually healthy Christian is a hungry Christian. This solves the problem of why so many children of God have so little love for the Word.[12] Some Christians live and treat others as if they have skipped their milk and therefore have forgotten the fundamental principles of the gospel. We must continue to desire and feed on God's Word because spiritual nourishment is essential to spiritual growth.

- If indeed you have tasted that the Lord is gracious – Here in 1 Peter 2:3, Paul is saying: *If so be*, or *since that*, or *forasmuch as, you have tasted that the Lord is gracious*. The apostle does not express a doubt but advises that all good Christians will have tasted the goodness of God, and hence argues with them that because they have, "You ought to lay aside these vile sins (v.1); you ought to desire the word of God; you ought to grow thereby, since you cannot deny that you have tasted that the Lord is gracious." By considering what is being

---

[12] Wuest, K. S. (1997). <u>*Wuest's word studies from the Greek New Testament: for the English reader*</u> (Vol. 11, pp. 51–52). Grand Rapids: Eerdmans.

said to us about our Lord and Savior Jesus Christ, and having had a taste of His grace, we learn, (1) Our Lord Jesus Christ is very gracious to his people. He is in himself infinitely good; he is very kind, free, and merciful to miserable sinners; he is pitiful and good to the undeserving; he has in him a fulness of grace. (2) The graciousness of our Redeemer is best discovered by an experimental taste of it. There must be an immediate application of this grace to your spiritual tongue; we cannot taste at a distance as we may see, hear, and smell. To taste the graciousness of Christ experimentally assumes our being united to him by faith, in close proximity to Him, and then we may taste his goodness in all his providences, in all our spiritual concerns, in all our fears and temptations, in His word and our worship of Him every day. (3) The best of God's servants have in this life but a taste of the grace of Christ. A taste is but a little; it is not a complete satisfaction of the thirst, nor does it satisfy. You know that there is more to be realized. (4) The word of God is the great instrument whereby He discovers and communicates His grace to men. Those who feed upon the sincere milk of the word taste and experience most of his grace. In our interactions with His word, we should endeavor always to understand and experience more and more of his grace.[13]

---

[13] Henry, M. (1994). *Matthew Henry's commentary on the whole Bible: complete and unabridged in one volume* (pp. 2425–2426). Peabody: Hendrickson.

- Verse 4 then says, "Coming to Him as to a living stone, rejected indeed by men, but chosen by God and precious" — As always, Peter begins with the Lord. The status of Christians depends upon the status of Christ, for they are joined to him. That is why as the body of believers is joined to Him, division and separation disappear. How striking it is that Peter names Christ the *Stone!* Peter's given name was Simon. It was Jesus who named him Cephas (in Greek, Peter), the 'rock.' Peter gratefully used the name Jesus gave him as an apostle (1:1). But Peter points us, not to himself, but to Christ as our Rock.[14] Only one edifice can stand against the storm of destruction: God's building, established upon one sure foundation stone. It is this figure that Jesus used when he said to Peter that the gates of hell could not prevail against his church. In the word of Jesus, He was himself the builder and Peter an apostolic rock of foundation; in the figure that Peter takes from Isaiah, Christ is the *precious* and tested *cornerstone.*[15]

- Verse 5 says, "You also, as living stones, are being built up a spiritual house, a holy priesthood, to offer up spiritual sacrifices acceptable to God through Jesus Christ…" Having described Christ as the foundation, the apostle goes on to speak of the superstructure, the

[14] Clowney, E. P. (1988). *The message of 1 Peter: the way of the cross* (p. 83). Leicester, England; Downers Grove, IL: InterVarsity Press.

[15] Clowney, E. P. (1988). *The message of 1 Peter: the way of the cross* (pp. 83–84). Leicester, England; Downers Grove, IL: InterVarsity Press.

materials built upon Him: *You also, as living stones, are built up.* The apostle is recommending the Christian church and constitution to these dispersed Jews. It was natural for them to object that the Christian church had no such glorious temple nor such a numerous priesthood, but its dispensation substituted all of that, the services and sacrifices of it having nothing of the pomp and grandeur which the Jewish dispensation had.

To this, the apostle answers that the Christian church is a much nobler fabric than the Jewish temple; it is a living temple, consisting not of dead materials but of living parts. Christ, the foundation, is a living stone. Christians are lively stones, and these make a spiritual house, and they are a holy priesthood; and, though they have no bloody sacrifices of beasts to offer, yet they have much better and more acceptable, and they have an altar too on which to present their offerings; for they offer spiritual sacrifices, acceptable to God by Jesus Christ.

It was by the realization of all this that the Christian of Peter's day and that we today learn the following: (1) All sincere Christians have in them a principle of spiritual life communicated to them from Christ their head (all believers; it is in this that the denominational separation loses its meaning): therefore, as Christ is called a living stone, so they are called lively, or living stones; not dead in trespasses and sins, but alive to God by regeneration and the working of the divine Spirit. (2) The church of God is a spiritual house. The foundation is Christ, Eph. 2:22. It is a house recognized for its strength, beauty, variety of parts, and usefulness of the whole. It is a spiritual foundation, Christ Jesus in the materials of it – spiritual persons, in its furniture – the graces of the Spirit, <u>in its connection – being held together by the Spirit of God and by one common faith</u>, and in its use, which is spiritual work – to offer up spiritual sacrifices.

It is this house, designed and conceived in heaven before the worlds were created, that is the pre-problem solution. In the councils of the Holy Trinity, not only was the creation of the earth conceived, but also this spiritual house that would lead fallen mankind, in all its variations, to live as one in Christ Jesus. And what I rejoice in today is that this house is daily being built up, every part of it improving, and the whole supplied in every age by the addition of new particular members. (3) It is by this reality that all true Christians are a holy priesthood. The apostle speaks here of the generality of Christians and tells them they are a holy priesthood; they are all select persons, sacred to God, serviceable to others, well endowed with heavenly gifts and graces, and well employed. (4) This holy priesthood must and will offer up spiritual sacrifices to God. Anything else, of any other construction, consisting of division and separation and envy and dissension, cannot offer up spiritual sacrifices that are acceptable to God. The spiritual sacrifices which Christians are to offer are their bodies, souls, affections, prayers, praises, alms, and other duties. (5) The most spiritual sacrifices of the best men are not acceptable to God, but through Jesus Christ; he is the only great high priest, through whom we and our services can be accepted; therefore, bring all your oblations to Him, and by Him present them to God.[16]

As we bring this chapter to a close, I pray that we now understand what God has provided us. His great plan of salvation, depicted by Paul as a spiritual house with Jesus Christ as the cornerstone, intends for us as living stones to be fitly joined together, not divided. It is my prayer, as we go forward, that we understand and embrace this reality and that it will affect how we relate to one another as children of God.

I close with this prayer: Build up this great house, O God, according to Your great plan, and may all who love you, regardless of the spoke they are currently on, find their place within its walls and enjoy the fellowship of the great family of God. Let it be so, in Jesus' name, AMEN!!!

---

[16] Henry, M. (1994). _Matthew Henry's commentary on the whole Bible: complete and unabridged in one volume_ (p. 2426). Peabody: Hendrickson.

The Solution Lived Out

Let's continue to review what Peter says so that we can better understand how God intends for us to live together as believers. One theologian summarized 1 Peter 2:1-5 by stating that what Peter was insisting was that <u>all believers must learn that living life involves spiritual growth verified by positive daily relationships and activities</u>. General Douglas MacArthur focused on a similar perspective: "Life is a lively process of becoming. If you haven't added to your interest during the past year; if you are thinking the same thoughts, relating the same personal experiences, having the same predictable reactions, then rigor mortis of the personality has set in." My fear is that spiritual rigor mortis has set in among God's people. Many Christians have not added to their interest, are thinking the same thoughts, relaying the same personal experiences, and having the same predictable reactions to life – within the same denomination, with believers of other denominations, towards nonbelievers. Nothing has changed in years. Their thoughts, their opinions, their perspectives of life, and of others have remained the same. No growth whatsoever, indicating that spiritual rigor mortis of the personality has set in as a result of the death of their spiritual selves, which is caused by the broken God/man relationship.

As we look across society today, there are so many people who don't know Christ, that are turned off, disgusted, or even repulsed by Christianity. This opinion often exists because of what they see, hear and experience from those who say they are Christians but who, in reality, have a broken relationship with God and have experienced this death to their spiritual selves, characterized by the stiff, unchanging, immovable effects of spiritual rigor mortis that has set in.

Oh, but I have great hope because I believe that at this time in earth's history, Jesus is coming to the aide of His people, walking among the candlesticks, as seen in Revelation 1:12-13, among the church, to give His people life again. I compare what is happening now in Christianity to the story found in John 11, when Lazarus, one that Jesus loved dearly, had gotten sick. His sisters Mary and Martha had sent word for Jesus to come and heal him. I propose to you that Christianity has been sick for some time, sicker than many have realized – with symptoms such as the misrepresentation of God and His Word, divisiveness, hatred, and placing denominational identity above God's truth, loss of love, and more. Like Mary and Martha, many have been calling on Jesus to come and heal the church, the body of Christ. But like the Lazarus story, it appears that Jesus has delayed coming, so much so that his beloved, the church, the body of Christ, has died, and many have lamented that if Jesus had shown up sooner, the church wouldn't be in this dead state.

When both believers and nonbelievers look at the current state of Christianity, far too often, they see pastors and members being materialistic, immoral, clannish, divisive, unethical, mishandling the Word of God, and misrepresenting Him. And because it seems like it has been this way so long, not even a recognized movement of Jesus changes the perception of those looking on. They may continue to have a fear similar to what Martha had in John 11:39 that like Lazarus, the body of Christ has been dead so long that not only has rigor mortis set in but we have begun to stink – stinking thinking, stinking attitudes toward others, stinking personal experiences, stinking and predictable reactions to life – and it is making Christianity repulsive to others. And as we consider the way in which many who call themselves Christian have conducted themselves in the recent past, having seen them behave abhorrently regarding issues like abortion, alternative lifestyles, political differences, race relations, immigration, vaccines, mask-wearing, and voter fraud, which has led to people being assaulted and killed, clinics being bombed, and even storming the Nation's capital, it leaves us stunned and ashamed. That is why many perceive what is considered the appalling, offensive, repulsive stench of spiritual death present among the people of God.

But I believe that Jesus is showing up among His people today. He is desiring to resurrect those that are spiritually dead and stinking, and He is issuing the command, "Roll away the stone." He is making the same call to His beloved today that

He gave His beloved then – come forth! And just as there was a stirring in the tomb that day, there is a stirring among the body of Christ today, and His people are coming forth from dead places, shedding the institutional and denominational burial wrappings which have bound them for far too long. He is saying, "Loose them and let them go," remove the grave-clothes and set them free from those man-made rituals and traditions so that they can be alive and become one in Me. Our Savior is restoring to His people the vibrant life and love that He intended them to have, having a true, loving relationship with Him and with each other. This is how the God/man and the man/man relationship, and the body of Christ will be restored and made able to live out that pre-problem solution in its fullness.

God is all about relationship! We cannot go very far in life before we realize how important relationships are. In chapter one of 1 Peter, Peter put an exclamation point on the believer's relationship with God the Father. This relationship is never far from his mind or pen, but in this chapter, he carefully underlined the importance of positive relationships with one another. His premise is that those who have a secure relationship with the Father through Jesus Christ are on a path of spiritual growth and development. One of the crucial growth points on this path is how we reflect positively on the relationship we have with God. This reflection is not simply to be relegated to a verbal testimony or witness, but it takes form as we live day to day among our fellow Christians and before those who do

not know Christ. Certain attitudes and actions need to be surrendered from the believer's pattern of living, lest our testimony to others become tainted.

By establishing and maintaining the God/man relationship, we not only have a more fulfilled life, but the original
God/man interaction is renewed, where we have the privilege
to walk and talk with God, as Adam did in the Garden of Eden,
and we are able to receive heavenly insights into the secret
things of this world by the Word of God. Deuteronomy 29:29
says, "The secret things belong unto the LORD our God: but
those things which are revealed belong unto us and to our children forever, that we may do all the words of this law." It was
this principle, realized in the restoration of the God/man relationship, that positioned men of old to receive heavenly inspi-
ration that brought clarity to their present and their future.
From Daniel and Isaiah and Jeremiah and other prophets of
the Bible to prophets and servants of God in our day, God has
given His people insights into the meaning of the past, the present, and the future, so that we can be assured of His ultimate
plan to save mankind.

God is true to His word found in Amos 3:7 which says,
"Surely the Lord GOD does nothing, until he reveals His secret
to His servants the prophets." Jesus reiterated this in John
15:15 when He said, "No longer do I call you servants, for a
servant does not know what his master is doing; but I have
called you friends, for all things that I heard from My Father I
have made known to you." It was the realization of these Bible
promises that enabled mankind to know the meaning of

events from the time of prophets like Daniel down through the ages to our time. It is also instrumental that we understand how the occurrence of certain events provides great insight into how we can better live out God's pre-problem solution, show greater love to all believers, and have a greater impact in our world today.

Prophecy, as presented in God's Word, has confirmed that God has provided a clear revelation of the occurrence and meaning of historical events and signs and wonders to explain the progression of time leading up to the full redemption of mankind. Using the Seventh-day Adventist Church as an example, we can see how a denomination came into existence, and through speculation, come to a realization of what could have happened during that time. In the 1800s, the fulfillment of certain celestial and terrestrial signs, predicted in the Bible, began a religious revival known as the **Second Great Awakening** in North America, South America, Europe, and Australia. An example of the spiritual revival in North America is seen through the works of the **Advent Movement**, pioneered by the Baptist minister, William Miller. Miller and <u>other advent members from various mainline Protestant denominations</u> that together began reading and studying the prophecies of Daniel and the Revelation, including the prophecies of Revelation Chapter 14. Through their studies, they came to understand that Christ's Second Coming and the end of the world were imminent.

By the year 1832, Miller and other supporters of the advent movement understood and taught that Jesus would return during the Hebrew calendar year, 1843. Basing their prediction on the prophecy recorded in Daniel 8:14, foretelling a sanctuary being cleansed after a prophetic period of 2,300 days, as well as the warning of judgment found in the First Angel's message of Revelation 14, they believed the earth and its inhabitants to be that sanctuary. In his book, "Grace On Trial," Robert Wieland states that it was from this understanding of prophecy that the name "Adventist" was born, identifying a people who believe that Christ's second coming is near. More than that, the name means one who loves the thought that it is near.

The Seventh-day Adventist Church sprang from a phenomenal conviction in the hearts of some humble Christians who discovered in the Bible a prophetic road map. To them, Daniel and Revelation revealed that mankind's weary journey in this world of sin was about at its end. To them, this was great Good News. The roots of the Adventist church go back to when <u>many Christians of different denominations</u> first saw these prophetic books as "unsealed." Of this group, Wieland writes, "Their hearts were in union with Christ. Because they sensed some appreciation for His character of love, they wanted Him to return. For that group of Christians from many different churches, there was no self-centered motivation to cloud the bright flame of their devotion to Christ.

The 1840s movement was thus the first time since the apostles where Jesus could find a community of believers on earth whose hearts were knit with His in joyful expectation of His soon return. They were among those of whom Jesus said,

"Blessed are they that have not seen, and yet have believed." This is why devotion similar to that of Pentecost marked them. It leaped across the centuries like fire blown by the wind. Joseph Bates spent his life savings spreading the message so that he came to face old age nearly penniless. Uriah Smith gave up a promising career for the toil and privations of Adventist editing. His sister Annie prematurely burned out the strength of her youth. Others sold farms and gave the proceeds to the cause. Young people such as the Loughboroughs and James and Ellen White threw themselves wholeheartedly into sacrificial living. The taste of this kind of Adventism was in their "mouth sweet as honey." Wow, this is a true picture of what prophetic revelation does for those who receive it.

However, there was an initial misinterpretation of prophecy by this group, in which they thought that the end of the 2300-day prophecy indicated the coming of Jesus instead of Him moving from the holy to the most holy place in the heavenly sanctuary. This led them to experience what is called the Great Disappointment. But instead of abandoning the study of God's Word, a core group dug deeper and discovered the truth, which galvanized their beliefs and made the beauty of prophecy even sweeter. But the Adventist message began to focus so much on end-time themes that the love of Christ became lost. It was then that the message of A.T. Jones and E.J. Waggoner at the 1888 General Conference in Minneapolis of the then infant Seventh-day Adventist denomination brought the focus back to righteousness by faith. Listen to how Ellen White responded to their message in her book, Testimonies to

Ministers, p. 91, 92 – "The Lord in His great mercy sent <u>a most precious message</u> to His people through Elders Waggoner and Jones. This message was to bring more prominently before the world the uplifted Savior, the sacrifice for the sins of the whole world. It presented justification through faith in the Surety; it invited the people to receive the righteousness of Christ, which is made manifest in obedience to all the commandments of God."

Here is what Wieland wrote: "No one can read our history and doubt that God has entrusted to this people His last message of grace for the world. It was ordained to supply a final cure for the problem of deep-rooted sin, producing a beautiful change in believing humanity, evidence that the sacrifice of Christ was not in vain. He defeated Satan at the cross, but now He must be glorified in His people. Satan's accusations must be forever silenced. The "most precious message" the Lord sent us was more than a thunder-and-lightning denunciation of sin abounding; it was a heart-warming revelation of grace much more abounding, a final reconciliation of alienated human hearts to God and to His holy law. It would capture the full devotion of every honest heart worldwide. The righteousness Christ accomplished in Himself would be displayed again in a generation of people who would "follow the Lamb whithersoever He goeth." But listen to what Wieland also wrote: "Adventism is the movement that should have brought fruition to two thousand years of Christianity. It was to complete the arrested Protestant Reformation of the sixteenth century and recover the truths that even John and Charles Wesley in the eighteenth century could not quite touch with their fingertips."

What we must recognize is that the advent movement of the 1800s was an interdenominational movement. God brought this about in an effort to establish unity by focusing on His truth. Through this experience, we see a group of believers with a focus on the truth of God instead of a focus on their denominations, and it led them to become one in Christ. Let me reemphasize this – truth above denomination. And it established relationships that furthered the kingdom of God. Can that be our experience today?

Let us consider critical points that must be recognized, and principles that must be applied that will enable us to see what living out God's solution should look like, and that could possibly allow an experience such as that of the 1800s to be repeated:

- ❖ Relationship sins are serious violations of God's grace.

- ❖ An individual either comes to Christ or rejects him— there is no middle ground.

- ❖ Jesus Christ is the centerpiece of the Christian church.

- ❖ Christians are a people whom God should possess.

- ❖ The Christian is to be an instrument that publicizes the attributes and character of God.

- ❖ God's grace gift of salvation must result in a positive change in the believer's behavior.

❖ God's desire for believers is that they submit to human governments.

❖ Christian freedom is not the freedom to do as we like; it is the freedom to do as we *ought*.

❖ Submission to those in authority should be done in a spirit of reverence toward God.

❖ The consciousness of the presence of God enables us to endure unjust suffering.

❖ Jesus Christ alone has provided atonement for our sins.

❖ Here are how those principles are applied:

❖ Spiritual growth should be a high priority for believers.

❖ Believers should make progress in dealing with anger, hatred, hypocrisy, envy, and slander.

❖ Do not say anything about other believers in their absence that you would not say to them personally.

❖ Unity should characterize the relationships and interactions of those who follow Jesus Christ.

❖ The believer is to proclaim the excellencies of Jesus Christ.

❖ Every Christian should be a good advertisement for Christianity.

❖ Moral purity is a mark of excellence in behavior.

- ❖ Christians must model a healthy respect and support for those in authority.

- ❖ Christians enjoy their liberty in Jesus Christ, realizing that this is not a license to do as they please.

- ❖ Christians may have to endure unjust suffering and should do so in the spirit and example of Jesus.

- ❖ Christians should resist the temptation to plot revenge toward others.[17]

1 Corinthians 12:12–26 shows how the body of believers should work together. "For as the body is one and has many members, but all the members of that one body, being many, are one body, so also is Christ. <u>For by one Spirit we were all baptized into one body—whether Jews or Greeks, whether slaves or free—and have all been made to drink [a]into one Spirit.</u> For in fact the body is not one member but many. If the foot should say, "Because I am not a hand, I am not of the body," is it therefore not of the body? And if the ear should say, "Because I am not an eye, I am not of the body," is it therefore not of the body? If the whole body were an eye, where would be the hearing? If the whole were hearing, where would be the smelling? But now God has set the members, each one of them, in the body just as He pleased. And if they were all one member, where would the body be? But now indeed there are many members, yet one body. And the eye cannot say to

---

[17] Walls, D., & Anders, M. (1999). *I & II Peter, I, II & III John, Jude* (Vol. 11, pp. 38–39). Nashville, TN: Broadman & Holman Publishers.

the hand, "I have no need of you"; nor again the head to the feet, "I have no need of you." No, much rather, those members of the body which seem to be weaker are necessary. And those members of the body which we think to be less honorable, on these we bestow greater honor; and our unpresentable parts have greater modesty, but our presentable parts have no need. But God composed the body, having given greater honor to that part which lacks it, that there should be no schism in the body, but that the members should have the same care for one another. And if one member suffers, all the members suffer with it; or if one member is honored, all the members rejoice with it."

Like at Pentecost, like in 1888, we today must get back to that spirit that supersedes denominations, where all God's people are drawn together by His truth. It can happen, it will happen, and I praise God for His Spirit that will draw all His people towards Him, closing the gap and making us one in Him.

The Community of Believers

So, what could it look like when God's people join together in unity? Psalms 133:1 says, "Behold, how good and how pleasant it is for brethren to dwell together in unity!" and I believe that the good and pleasant relationship of God's people can be realized today in spite of all the divisiveness and ugliness that we presently see. We must stretch our understanding of what makes us this community, the body of Christ, God's own special people. Consider what comes to mind when you think of the ideal community. Depending on whether you have an urban or a rural preference, there are certain elements of an ideal community that exist regardless, things like friendly neighbors, a pleasant environment, and access to basic needs such as grocery stores, gas stations, hospitals, etc. You also want to have a well-functioning municipality that will pick up the trash, clear snow from the roads, and keep the utilities up and running. And with every ideal community, there is the concern about who moves in and whether they will help maintain and enhance the community or whether they will change it for the worse.

There may be many things that may come to mind when you think about being a part of an ideal community, and in the context of this chapter, I ask that you consider what characteristics should exist in the ideal community of believers. As we think about this, let's also consider whether we are being good neighbors that are enhancing the community of believers, leading to unity and oneness in Christ Jesus, or whether we are changing it for the worse. I feel that it is important for us to consider this because sometimes I wonder if we are even considering what kind of neighbors we are in this community of believers. Are we being friendly to other believers? Are we welcoming them to the community? Just like any other community, people may live in different houses and may come from different cultures with different practices and customs, and preferences, but they are still a part of our community. So, how are we treating them?

Let's relook at the text we studied in the previous chapter found in 1 Corinthians 12 NKJV, and as we read verses 12–13, let's consider what it means in the context of the community of believers. It reads, "For as the body is one and has many members, but all the members of that one body, being many, are one body, so also is Christ. <u>For by one Spirit we were all baptized into one body—whether Jews or Greeks, whether slaves or free—and have all been made to drink into one Spirit</u>." Now, consider what this text does to our thinking if we were to use it to assist us in understanding the dynamics of the all-inclusive community of believers. It would help us to understand that the body spoken of here was not just our specific church or denomination, but it was speaking of the community of believers.

Now, let's look at this text in the New Living Translation so that we can see it in plain English. It says, "Our own body has many parts. When all these many parts are put together, they are only one body. The body of Christ is like this. [13] It is the same way with us (the body of believers). Jews or those who are not Jews, men who are owned by someone, or men who are free to do what they want to do, have all been baptized into the one body by the same Holy Spirit. We have all received the one Spirit," or as the King James Version says, "have all been made to drink into one Spirit." It is verse 13 that I believe has caused many to be confused about who is a part of the community of believers. Notice the text says, that by one Spirit, we were all baptized into one body, whether Jew or Greeks, whether slaves or free. This means that even though believers, like people in a community, may come from different backgrounds and have different cultures and practices and experiences and understandings, all those who have accepted Jesus as their Savior were all baptized into one body. This concept is challenged in many of our churches today.

In every Christian congregation, we have people who read the same Bible, who accept the Lord Jesus as their Savior, who are baptized and become members, but because of their cultures and practices and experiences and understandings, we have some who eat meat and some who don't, some who keep the Sabbath one way and some who keep it another way, some who understand prophecy one way and some another. And what is the ideal response to this? In love and fellowship as a church family, there should be seminars and preaching series and prayer meetings, and Sabbath/Sunday School so that through the study of God's Word, we grow together in the knowledge of God's truth. And the church grows stronger, and we become a better witness to the world around us.

Now, imagine if we expanded what we do in our individual churches to the community of believers. Imagine if we stopped identifying our neighbors across the street or across town as nonbelievers or Sunday/Saturday worshipers and instead recognized them as our neighbors in the community of believers that simply come from different backgrounds and cultures and practices and experiences and understandings. Imagine if we recognized that we all have been baptized into the one body by the same Holy Spirit, and therefore have all been "made to drink into one Spirit."

I believe we will find, just like in our own congregations, people who read the same Bible, who accept the Lord Jesus as their Savior and are baptized, but because of their cultures and practices and experiences and understandings, may eat differently than we do, and worship differently than we do, and understand prophecy differently than we do. And they love the Lord just as much as we do. Then what should we do? Imagine if in love and fellowship as a community of believers, instead of separating from each other and giving each other labels such as unbelievers and Sunday/Saturday worshipers, we together participated in preaching series and prayer meetings and Sabbath/Sunday Schools and seminars so that through the study of God's Word we would grow together in the knowledge of God's truth. Imagine if we had the spirit of the early church in Acts and the advent movement in the 1800s, and we allowed the focus to be on the truth of God instead of on our denominational differences. Then the true church, the body of Christ, the community of believers would grow stronger and become a better witness to the world around us. Then we would be one in Him, and what Jesus prayed to His Father in John 17 would come true—"The world would know that thou have sent Me."

Now that we understand this, we can ask ourselves if we are being good neighbors in this community of believers, or do we think that our particular denomination has a monopoly on Christianity and don't have to worry about whether we are enhancing the community of believers, but instead think that everyone should be like us. As you ponder this, I direct you to another section of scripture that provides an excellent blueprint for this community of believers. Ephesians 4:1-6, 13 says, "I, therefore, the prisoner of the Lord, beseech you to walk worthy of the calling with which you were called, with all lowliness and gentleness, with longsuffering, bearing with one another in love, <u>endeavoring to keep the unity of the Spirit in the bond of peace</u>. There is one body and one Spirit, just as you were called in one hope of your calling; one Lord, one faith, one baptism; one God and Father of all, who is above all, and through all, and in you all. <u>Till we all come in the unity of the faith</u>, and of the knowledge of the Son of God, unto a perfect man, unto the measure of the stature of the fulness of

Christ." It is in this section of scripture that we find important elements that will enable us to be good neighbors in the community of believers, and I believe that it is important for us to analyze this so that we can be sure that we are following God's blueprint.

❖ Walk worthy of the calling with which you were called – we must recognize that it is a privilege and an honor to be a part of the family of God, to have been called out of darkness into this marvelous light. The SDA Commentary says that it is impossible to be entirely worthy of our calling, but one may be continually under the leading of God. God has not called us because we are worthy, for worthiness follows the call. No man would ever be called of God if it depended on his worthiness. The Ephesians, who were once aliens and foreigners, but who have now been united into one body with God's formerly chosen people and have received the promises of God, are called upon to exhibit certain visible evidence of that gracious change. To walk the Christian way means more than concern about separate acts of outward conduct; it relates to an inner condition and attitude that provides the motivating force behind the acts. It is in walking worthy of this calling that will enable us to love and accept our neighbors in the community of believers as part of the family of God.

❖ With all lowliness and gentleness, with longsuffering – this refers to us as Christians having unselfish humility, being able to accept the trials of life and the faults of others with grace and being patient under any and all conditions. These qualities are essential to the unity in the church and in the community of believers.

❖ Bearing with one another in love – the quality is manifested only by a heart that loves like Jesus loves, a love that includes all mankind.

❖ Endeavoring to keep the unity of the Spirit in the bond of peace – this means that we are earnestly striving for oneness, a quality that is given by the Holy Spirit. It cannot be generated by the flesh, only from above.

❖ There is one body and one Spirit, just as you were called in one hope of your calling – this begins a sevenfold repetition of the word "one." Unity is the apostle's theme in these verses. There are many members, but one body. The Christian is not a solitary pilgrim; he belongs to a vital organism, the family of God. This unit replaces the state, the club, and even the human family as the supreme object of his attachment. The One Spirit spoken of here is the source from which all gifts, fruits, and graces of the Christian life that come by its indwelling presence in the personal lives of believers and thus the church, the community of believers. And the one hope is the hope of salvation and the appearance of the Lord. It is the hope of the final consummation of the kingdom that gives a substantial basis for peace and joy, courage, and good cheer.

- One Lord, one faith, one baptism – those who give complete submission and allegiance to the same Lord are not at enmity with one another. Utter surrender to Him is a requirement, but such a surrender will be the Christian's greatest joy. One faith, which is in Christ Jesus as a personal savior rather than a faith as an arbitrary system. One baptism, by water which aptly symbolizes death and resurrection, cleansing and separation, and a public announcement of union with the body of Christ.

- One God and Father of all, who is above all, and through all, and in you all – speaks to our shared origin, the hub to which all believers are connected.

- Till we all come in the unity of the faith, and of the knowledge of the Son of God, unto a perfect man, unto the measure of the stature of the fulness of Christ—this is what will make the community of believers such a wonderful place, a place where all believers, regardless of background and culture and ethnicity, live in unity. Are we preparing ourselves to be good neighbors in this community? By God's grace, yes, we are.

John 8:31–32 says, 31 "Then Jesus said to those Jews who believed Him, 'If you abide in My word, you are My disciples indeed. 32 And you shall know the truth, and the truth shall make you free.'"

If we abide, continue, and keep studying God's Word, then we become His true, sure enough disciples (indeed). It is then that we will know the truth more completely, and that truth will make us truly free, free from the bounds of man-made structures (denominationally) that leave us separated and moves us to where we can become one in Him.

Mark 4:24 says, "Then He said to them, 'Take heed what you hear. With the same measure you use, it will be measured to you; and to you who hear, more will be given.'" Take heed/take note of what you hear as you stay in God's Word. However much of God's Word you use, that much and more will be measured to you, and to those who hear/follow/apply/use/obey God's Word, God will measure more and give it to you.

John 10:16 says, "And other sheep I have which are not of this fold; them also I must bring, and they will hear My voice; and there will be one flock *and* one shepherd. There is only one way to God." Jesus said to him, "I am the way, the truth, and the life. No one comes to the Father except through Me." And as we as one flock follow one shepherd, we will be better able to grow together and walk together and share together and study together. It will impact how we engage in what we often call 'sharing our faith.'

It should be recognized that there are certain doctrinal truths that are particular to certain denominations, such as the Three Angels Messages of Revelation 14 promoted by the Seventh-day Adventist Church. However, it is also important that the understanding of these truths does not mean that they can be claimed or owned by that denomination. It only means that they have been favored to receive a glorious fraction of the multifaceted light that emanates from the throne/Word of God, light that is owned by and belongs only to God. And whatever light received is to be shared with gratitude and great humility with the world, giving glory and honor to the One from whence it comes, not claimed by the recipient of that light as a means of proclaiming some theological exclusivity or denominational preeminence.

The Gospel, the faith of Jesus Christ, is not ours as in owned or possessed by us, to be shared with others like gifts from the wealthy to the less fortunate. That creates a very wrong and improper dynamic and esthetic. Whatever rays of the multifaceted light of the Gospel are possessed by the Christian only because they have been favored to have been shown it by the Holy Spirit, and they must graciously and gratefully receive and accept it as a gift from their benevolent Father. And the Christian is to, therefore, share it with excitement, gratitude, and humility because we recognize it as a gift given and not a possession to be claimed. Then, in the sharing of these glorious fractions of light with one another, combining and studying them together, the Holy Spirit will hover over this marvelous laboratory of loving Christian brotherhood as He did during creation, bringing order to what was once chaotic, 'Without form and void.' Then the preparation will be made for the Creator to proclaim, "Let there be light," and the shared light received by the community of believers will become a glorious beacon, "The prophetic word confirmed, which you do well to heed as a light that shines in a dark place,

until the day dawns and the morning star rises in your hearts"
(II Peter 1:19 NKJV).

May we all who are a part of the community of believers
establish the Word of God as the platform for unity, not the
foundation for division. Let us apply the Steven Covey approach and begin all theological discussion with the end in
mind, to become one in Him, so that the world may believe,
by our unity, that He, the Word made flesh, was sent by God
(John 17:21). It is then that the glory which God gave His Son
will be given to and seen in us, the worldwide family of God,
as we become one just as the Father and the Son are one (John
17:22).

The Real Lord's Prayer

The previous chapter may have seemed like an unreachable dream as we visualized what the community of believers could look like. The whole idea of people of different cultures and practices and experiences and understandings coming together in the spirit of the early church in Acts and of the founders of the Seventh-day Adventist church, studying and praying and worshiping and praying and studying together until the truth made them one in Christ Jesus seems remarkable. So, in an effort to understand what makes this occurrence plausible, let's take a step back and analyze the prayer that Jesus prayed in John 17, what I call "The Real Lord's Prayer." My hope is that by looking closely at this prayer, we and all other believers will gain confidence and strength from the fact that because <u>Jesus</u> prayed this prayer for us, it can be our reality.

In the "Lord's Prayer" in Matt. 6, Jesus sets forth what His disciples should desire for themselves. But in His prayer in

John 17, He indicates what He desires for them.[18] Following
the symbolic washing of the disciples' feet in John 13:1–30 and
His private instruction of the apostles in chapters 14–16, Jesus
prayed this prayer found in John 17, which has been called
"the Lord's high-priestly prayer," and "the Lord's prayer." Jesus had ended His teaching of the disciples with a shout of victory: "I have overcome the world" (16:33). This was in antici-
pation of His work on the cross. Throughout His ministry, Jesus' work was done in obedience to the Father's will (cf. Luke
4:42; 6:12; 11:1; Matt. 26:36). As He turned again to His Father, He prayed first for Himself (John 17:1–5), then for His
apostles (vv. 6–19), and finally for future believers (vv. 20–
26).[19] In Matthew Henry's Commentary of the Whole Bible,
we find that there is a specific and purposeful transition in Jesus' prayer. Next to the purity of His people, he prays for their
unity, for the wisdom that the believer receives from above is
first pure, providing purity to believers, then peaceable, which
provides unity to believers. This is the first big benefit all believers receive because of this prayer – purity and unity. And
the goodwill and friendship that comes as a result of the presence of purity and unity in the community of believers are
available in abundance because Jesus prayed this prayer. It is
like the ointment on Aaron's holy head and the dew on Zion's

[18] Vincent, M. R. (1887). *Word studies in the New Testament* (Vol. 2, p. 262). New
York: Charles Scribner's Sons.

[19] Blum, E. A. (1985). John. In J. F. Walvoord & R. B. Zuck (Eds.), *The Bible
Knowledge Commentary: An Exposition of the Scriptures* (Vol. 2, pp. 330–331).
Wheaton, IL: Victor Books.

holy hill. There are several things that we can observe in this prayer:

1. <u>The first thing we can observe is who is included in this prayer (v. 20):</u> "Not these only," "not these only that are now my disciples" (the eleven, the seventy, with others, men and women that followed him when he was here on earth), "but for those also who shall believe on me through their word," referring to either the words preached by them in their own day or written by them in scripture for the generations to come; I pray for them all, that they all may be one in their interest in this prayer, and may all receive benefit by it." You can see here how all-encompassing this prayer is. Also, note here that this refers to:

   a. Those, and those only, that are interested in the mediation of Christ, that do, or shall, believe in him. This belief in Jesus is that by which they are described, and it comprehends all the character and duty of a Christian. They that lived then, saw and believed, but all who lived after Bible times that have not seen, were not eyewitnesses, and yet have believed.

   b. It is through the Word, that souls are brought to believe in Christ, and it is for this end that Christ appointed the scriptures to be written and a standing ministry to continue in the church while the church stands, that is, while the world stands, for the spreading the gospel and the raising up of a seed.

c. It is certainly and unfailingly known to Christ who shall believe in Him. He does not here pray at a venture, with uncertainty as to the outcome, upon a contingency depending on the treacherous will of man, which pretends to be free, but by reason of sin is in bondage with its children; no, Christ knew very well who He was praying for; the matter was reduced to a certainty by His divine foresight and purpose; He knew who was given to Him, who was being ordained to eternal life, entered in the Lamb's book, and should undoubtedly believe. Acts 13:48 says, "Now when the Gentiles heard this, they were glad and glorified the word of the Lord. And as many as had been appointed in eternal life believed."

d. Jesus Christ intercedes not only for great and eminent believers, but for the meanest and weakest; not for those only that are to be employed in the highest post of trust and honor in his kingdom, but for all, even those that in the eye of the world are inconsiderable. It is this point that enables us to have trust in the community of believers. All who believe in Jesus are included. As the divine providence extends itself to the meanest creature, so does the divine grace to the meanest Christian. The Good Shepherd has an eye even for the poor of the flock. This is what was spoken in Hebrews 8:11 in describing the new covenant. It says, "For all shall know Me, from the least of them to the greatest of them."

e. Jesus Christ, in this prayer, had an actual regard for those of the chosen remnant that were yet unborn, the people that should be created. Ps. 22:31 NKJV says, "They will come and declare His righteousness to a people who will be born, that He has done this," the other sheep which he must yet bring. Please let's understand this. Jesus' prayer covered believers that were yet to be born and those other sheep that He must yet bring in. Before they were formed in the womb, He knows them (Jer. 1:5), and prayers are filed in heaven for them beforehand by Him who declares the end from the beginning and calls things that are not as though they were.

So, we see that it is not for us to try to define who is included in Jesus' prayer as He prays for all believers, and it is not for us to try to determine who should and should not belong to the community of believers, for this prayer covers not only the least to the greatest but even those that are not yet born.

2. <u>The second thing we can observe is what is intended in this prayer (John 17:21):</u> *That they all may be one.* The same was said before of the disciples (*v.* 11), *that they may be one as we are,* and again of all believers in *v.* 22. The heart of Christ was focused much upon this. Some think that the oneness prayed for in *v.* 11 has special reference to the disciples as ministers and apostles, that they might be one in their testimony to Christ; and that the harmony of the evangelists, and concurrence of the first preachers of the

gospel, are owing to this prayer. Let them be not only of *one heart,* but of *one mouth,* speaking the same thing. The unity of the gospel ministers is both the beauty and strength of the gospel interest. But it is certain that the oneness prayed for in *v.* 21 respects and includes all believers. It is the prayer of Christ for all that are His, and we may be sure it is an answered prayer—*that they all may be one,* one in us (*v.* 21), one *as we are one* (*v.* 22), made *perfect in one, v.* 23. This oneness includes three things:

a. That they might all be *incorporated into one body.* "Father, look upon them all as one, and ratify that great charter by which they are embodied as one church. Though they live in distant places, from one end of heaven to the other, and in several ages, from the beginning to the close of time, and so cannot have any personal acquaintance or correspondence with each other, yet let them be united in Me, their common Head." As Christ died, so he prayed, to *gather them all in one.* Ephesians 1:10 NKJV says, "That in the dispensation of the fullness of the times He might gather in one all things in Christ, both which are in heaven, and which are on earth – in Him."

b. That they might all be *animated by one Spirit.* This is plainly implied in—*that they may be one in us.* Union with the Father and Son is obtained and kept up only by the Holy Ghost. 1 Corinthians 6:17 NKJV says, "But he who is joined to the Lord is one spirit with Him."

Let them all be stamped with the same image and superscription and influenced by the same power.

c. That they might all be *knit together* in the bond of love and charity, all of one heart. *That they all may be one,*

(1) One in judgment and sentiment; not in every little thing, like the self-proclaimed details of the Pharisees and the Jews and the denominations of today, for this is neither possible nor needful, but in the great things of God, and in them, by the virtue of this prayer, they are all agreed – that God's favor is better than life, that sin is the worst of evils, that Christ is the best friend you can have, that there is another life after this, and the like.

(2) One in disposition and inclination. All that are sanctified have the same divine nature and image; they all have a new heart, and it is *one heart.*

(3) They are all one in their designs and aims. Every true Christian, *as far as he is so,* eyes the glory of God as his highest end, and the glory of heaven as his chief good.

(4) They are all one in their desires and prayers; though they differ in words and the manner of expressions, yet, having received the same *spirit of adoption,* and observing the same rule, they pray for the same things in effect.

(5) All one in love and affection. Every true Christian has that in him which inclines him to love all true Christians as such. That which Christ here prays for is that *communion of saints* which we profess to believe; the fellowship which all believers have with God, the existence of the community of believers, and their intimate union with all the saints in heaven and earth spoken of in 1 John 1:3. But this prayer of Christ will not have its complete answer till all the saints come to heaven, for then, and not till then, they shall be *perfect in one*, as v. 23 says. Ephesians 4:13 NKJV says, "Till we all come to the unity of the faith and of the knowledge of the Son of God, to a perfect man, to the measure of the stature of the fullness of Christ."

3. The third thing we can observe in this prayer is what Jesus' intended purpose was by pleading for the implementation of this petition; let's consider three things that Jesus' deeply desired:

    a. The oneness that is between the Father and the Son, which is mentioned, again and again, v. 11, 21–23. (1) It is taken for granted that the Father and Son are one, one in nature and essence, equal in power and glory, and one in mutual endearments. The *Father loveth the Son*, and the Son always pleased the Father. They are one in design and one in operation. The intimacy of this oneness is expressed in these words, *thou in me, and I in thee*. This He often mentions for His support under His present sufferings, when His enemies were ready to fall upon Him, and His friends to fall off from Him; yet He was in the Father and the Father in Him.

b. This is insisted on in Christ's prayer for His disciples' oneness for three reasons:

1. As the pattern of that oneness, showing how He desired they might be one. Believers are one in some measure as God and Christ are one; for, *First*, the union of believers is a strict and close union; they are united by a divine nature, by the power of divine grace, in pursuance of the divine counsels. *Secondly*, it is a holy union, in the Holy Spirit, for holy ends, not a body politic for any secular purpose. *Thirdly*, it is and will be, at last, a complete union. Father and Son have the same attributes, properties, and perfections; so, have believers now, as far as they are sanctified, and when grace shall be perfected in glory, they will be exactly consonant to each other, all changed into the same image. Do you see how united Jesus wants the community of believers to be?

2. As the center of that oneness, that they may be *one in us*, in the unity of the Godhead (like the spokes in the wagon wheel, all meeting in the hub). There is *one God* and *one Mediator*; and herein believers are one, that they all agree to depend upon the favor of this one God as their joy and the merit of this one

Mediator as their righteousness. <u>Anything that does not center on God at its end, with Christ as the way, is a conspiracy, not a union.</u> All who are truly united to God and Christ, who *are one*, will soon be *united one to another*.

3. As a plea for that oneness. The Creator and Redeemer are one in interest and design; but what is the purpose of them being one if all believers are not one body with Christ and do not jointly receive grace for grace from him, as he has received it for them? <u>Christ's design was to reduce rebellious mankind to God into one entity</u>: In effect, Jesus is saying, "Father, let all that believe be one, that *in one body* they may be reconciled." Ephesians 3:15, 16 NKJV, which speaks of the uniting of Jews and Gentiles in the church, says, "From whom the whole family in heaven and earth is named, that He would grant you, according to the riches of His glory, to be strengthened with might through His Spirit in the inner man." That great mystery, that the Gentiles should be *fellow-heirs, and of the same body*, as spoken of in Ephesians 3:6, to which this prayer of Christ principally refers, it being one great thing he aimed for in his dying; "Father, let the Gentiles that believe be incorporated with the believing Jews, and *make of twain one new man*." Those words, *I in them, and thou in me*, show why this union is so necessary, not only to the beauty but to the very being,

of his church. *First,* Union with Christ: *I in them.* Christ dwelling in the hearts of believers is the life and soul of the new man. *Secondly,* Union with God through Him: *Thou in me,* so as by Me to be in them. *Thirdly,* Union with each other, resulting from these: *that they* hereby *may be made perfect in one.* We are complete in him.

4. The fourth and final thing we observe in this prayer is that Jesus pleads for the happy influence their oneness would have upon others and the persistent benefit it would give to the public good. This is twice urged (v. 21): *That the world may believe that thou hast sent me.* And again (v. 23): *That the world may know it,* for without knowledge there can be no true faith. Believers must know what they believe, and why and wherefore they believe it. Christ here shows,

   a. His goodwill to the world of mankind in general. In this, He is of the same mind as His Father, as we are sure He is in everything, that He would have all men to be saved and to *come to the knowledge of the truth,* as spoken of in 1 Timothy 2:4 and 2 Peter 3:9. Therefore it is His will that all means possible should be used, and no stone left unturned, for the conviction and conversion of the world. We don't know who is chosen, but we must, in our places, do our utmost to further men's salvation and avoid doing anything that would hinder it.

b. Christ in this prayer also shows the good fruit of the church's oneness; it will be evidence of the truth of Christianity and bring many to embrace it. The embodying of Christians in one society, one community of believers, by the gospel charter will greatly promote Christianity. When the world shall see so many of those that were once its children changed from what they once were by the foolishness of preaching (1 Corinthians 1:21) and kept up by miracles of divine providence and grace, and how admirably well it is modeled and constituted, they will be ready to say, *We will go with you, for we see that God is with you. Secondly,* the uniting of Christians in love and charity is the beauty of their profession and invites others to join with them, as the love that was among those primitive Christians talked about in Acts 2:42, 43; 4:32, 33.

When Christianity makes all other strifes and divisions cease – when it cools the fiery, smooths the rugged, and disposes men to be kind and loving, courteous and beneficent, to all men, it will draw people to it. In particular, it will produce in men good thoughts, *First*, Of Christ: They will know and believe that *thou hast sent me.* By this, it will appear that Christ was sent by God and that <u>his doctrine was divine, in that his religion prevails to join so many people of different capacities, tempers, beliefs, and interests in other things into one body by faith, with one heart by love.</u> *Secondly*, Of Christians: They will *know that thou hast loved them as thou hast loved me.* It will appear that God loves us if we *love one another with a pure heart;* for wherever *the love of God is shed abroad in the heart,* it will change it into the same image. See how much good it would do to the world to know better how dear to God all good Christians are. The Jews had a saying, "*If the world did but know the worth of good men, they would hedge them about with pearls.*" Those that have so much of God's love should have more of ours.[20]

I hope we all now see why Jesus prayed this prayer and all that He had in mind when He prayed it. My prayer for all believers, the community of believers, and the family of God is that this prayer becomes our reality. Let the love of God be evident in the community of believers. As we draw closer to Him, let us draw closer to one another until we become one in Him.

---

[20] Henry, M. (1994). *Matthew Henry's commentary on the whole Bible: complete and unabridged in one volume* (pp. 2033–2034). Peabody: Hendrickson.

Will Jesus' Prayer Ever Be Answered?

Now it is time for a reality check, for we have been considering some pretty lofty things thus far. This whole idea of us being one in Christ, of us living in unity in the community of believers, studying and praying and worshiping and praying and studying together until the truth makes us one in Him, —can that really happen? Let's be honest, as we look across the Christian landscape, we see how divided the body of believers presently is, how some people of different denominations don't associate with other believers, let alone live in unity. So, after spending time in the previous chapter thoroughly reviewing Jesus' prayer in John 17 and gaining a better understanding of the depth and essence of this prayer for unity, the question we must ask ourselves is posed in the title of this chapter – "Will Jesus' Prayer Ever Be Answered?" As I pondered and prayed and worried and wondered about this question, the Holy Spirit came to my rescue and assured me that I don't need to worry or wonder about whether Jesus' prayer would ever be answered. He let me know that it already has been answered, that the precedent has been set, and unity among believers has already taken place. Yes, it's been done before. The Spirit then showed me that not only has unity among believers happened before, but it will happen again before Jesus returns.

So, today we will look back at that time when unity among believers from different backgrounds and ethnicities and belief systems and understandings actually took place. We will take a close look at what the people did and what the Godhead did to allow Jesus' prayer to be answered during that time. Then we will consider what we must allow the Godhead to do, in order for Jesus' prayer to be answered among the community of believers during our time today.

As we identify and analyze the first time that Jesus' prayer was answered, we will do so by applying a threefold process. First, we will look at what was going on when Jesus' prayer was answered the first time. Then we will look at the people that were involved in Jesus' prayer being answered the first time. Then we will look at what the Godhead did to facilitate Jesus' prayer being answered the first time. After we have applied this threefold process to gain a better understanding of the first time Jesus' prayer was answered, we will then apply this same process to our time to get a better understanding of how Jesus' prayer <u>will</u> be answered in our time today. And my prayer is that after this review is done, we and believers everywhere will cooperate with the process so that this unity among the family of God, in the community of believers, will become our reality so that Jesus can come and take His people home. Let's get started.

First, let's look at the times in which Jesus' prayer was answered the first time. It was the time of the formation of the early church, which is found in scripture in Acts 1 and 2. The setting is right after the most horrific and disturbing experiences to believers had taken place – their Savior, the one whom they thought would save them from the oppressive Roman rule and establish His kingdom, had just been crucified. As we reflect on that time, we can only imagine how devastating the crucifixion of Christ must have been to the body of believers. Imagine the emotions they must have felt on that dreadful Friday evening and the following day. If we were able to transport ourselves mentally and emotionally back to that time, I'm sure we all would agree that our hearts would be broken and our minds extremely troubled by that event. But praise God, if we had been able to transport ourselves and join the believers of that time, we would not stay in that devasted state forever, for early on the third day, that Sunday morning, the unbelievable, unimaginable truth that Jesus had told them about actually took place. Hallelujah, Jesus rose from the dead!!!

Luke, the author of the book of Acts, wrote in chapter 1:3 that Jesus remained with the disciples for forty days, after which several amazing events took place—Jesus granted the disciples the promise of the Holy Spirit, then ascended back to

His Father in heaven; about 120 believers gathered in the upper room, chose Mathias as the replacement for Judas, stayed in that upper room until they became on one accord, then the promised Holy Spirit fell on the believers like cloven tongues of fire; Peter preached a sermon that won about 3,000 souls, and the body of believers not only grew, but they became united, one in Christ Jesus, or as Acts 2:44 NKJV says, "Now all who believed were together, and had all things in common."

For the historical setting of the book of Acts, according to the SDA Commentaries, the Roman Empire was enjoying its heyday during the years of A.D. 31–63. It further states that even though a number of emperors reigned during that time, some good and some evil, yet in spite of its checkered leadership, the empire maintained conditions that were favorable to the spreading of the gospel. Those conditions included a fairly stable government, a common administrative system, Roman justice, and an expanding citizenship, peace preserved by disciplined legions, roads pressing into every corner of the then-known world, and a language (Greek) that was almost universally understood. These factors favored the program undertaken by the apostles. Yes, it was truly an amazing time.

Now let's look at the people that were involved in Jesus' prayer being answered the first time and what they were doing. After witnessing Jesus' ascension, as described in Acts 1:9–11, the Eleven, together with Mary, the mother of Jesus, and with other women and men, return to Jerusalem and wait harmoniously in a second-floor room for the outpouring of

God's Spirit. Acts 1:14 NKJV says, "These all continued with one accord in prayer and supplication, with the women and Mary the Mother of Jesus, and with His brothers." Let's draw key points from this scripture – they did not gather in the temple where the disciples still worshiped, but in the upper story of a private house, where they would be in seclusion. This could suggest that for special things to happen, you can't be in the general crowd but in a private prayer meeting with those committed to following Christ— the disciples, the women that ministered to and had a close relationship with Christ, Jesus' mother, and His brothers (who had problems with Jesus during His ministry, who were not mentioned among those who gathered around the cross, but who now find themselves numbered among those who believe after all that has happened).

Acts 1:15–26 shows how this group goes about cooperating with heaven to choose a replacement for Judas (an example of how to approach making personnel moves in ministry). Then Acts 2:1–4 says that this group remained obedient to the instruction of Jesus by staying in that upper room until they received the promise. They couldn't rush this nor operate on their time. And when the Day of Pentecost had fully come, these 120 people, plus other believers who may have joined them, were all with one accord in one place.

Are you beginning to get a picture of what that community of believers looked like? It was then that the Holy Ghost fell on them like cloven tongues of fire, and its immediate manifestation was the gift of tongues. They were able to speak the gospel in the languages of everyone that was present in Jerusalem. Peter was able to preach a message that won over 3,000 people. Then Acts 2 ends with a critical and instructional description of the people that were involved when Jesus' prayer was answered the first time. It says, "And they continued steadfastly in the apostles' doctrine and fellowship, in the breaking of bread, and in prayers. Then fear came upon every soul, and many wonders and signs were done through the apostles. Now all who believed were together, and had all things in common, and sold their possessions and goods, and divided them among all, as anyone had need. So, continuing daily with one accord in the temple, and breaking bread from house to house, they ate their food with gladness and simplicity of heart, praising God and having favor with all the people. And the Lord added to the church daily those who were being saved." So, now we see what the people were like that were involved in Jesus' prayer when it was answered the first time.

Now let's look at what the Godhead was doing during this time when Jesus' prayer was answered the first time. We see this Triune God responding to Jesus' sacrifice on Calvary in a marvelous way. Acts 2:32–33 tells us how Peter, freshly anointed with the Holy Spirit, describes what had taken place in heaven: "This Jesus hath God raised up, whereof we all are witnesses. Therefore, being by the right hand of God exalted, and having received of the Father the promise of the Holy Ghost, he hath shed forth this, which ye now see and hear." God the Father received His Son back to the heavenly courts and acknowledged that Jesus had successfully accomplished His mission to secure the salvation of mankind.

The SDA Commentary says, "The great episodes in the incarnate life of Jesus, His birth, His baptism and reception of the Holy Spirit, His crucifixion, His resurrection, His ascension, were of supreme importance, and central to the unfolding plan of salvation. But the outpouring of the Spirit on the day of Pentecost followed upon the heavenly acceptance of Christ's great sacrifice and His enthronement with the Father. By that outpouring, the church was empowered to do for Christ what had never before been attempted, the preaching of the good news of salvation to all nations.[21] Ellen White, in Acts of the Apostles, p. 38–39, describes it this way, "When Christ passed within the heavenly gates, He was enthroned amidst the adoration of the angels. As soon as this ceremony was completed, the Holy Spirit descended upon the disciples in rich currents, and Christ was indeed glorified, even with the glory which He had with the Father from all eternity. The Pentecostal outpouring was Heaven's communication that the Redeemer's inauguration was accomplished. According to His promise, He had sent the Holy Spirit from heaven to His followers as a token that He had, as priest and king, received all authority in heaven and on earth, and was the Anointed One over His people.[22] And it was because of Heaven's response to

---

[21] Nichol, F. D. (Ed.). (1980). _The Seventh-day Adventist Bible Commentary_ (Vol. 6, p. 137). Review and Herald Publishing Association.

[22] White, E. G. (1911). _The Acts of the Apostles in the Proclamation of the Gospel of Jesus Christ_ (Vol. 4, pp. 38–39). Pacific Press Publishing Association.

Jesus' sacrifice that God's people received Holy Ghost power, thousands were saved in a day, and Acts 2 closes by describing the effects this unified community of believers had on that region. It says, "So, continuing daily with one accord in the temple, and breaking bread from house to house, they ate their food with gladness and simplicity of heart, praising God and having favor with all the people. And the Lord added to the church daily those who were being saved."

So, now that we have applied this threefold process to identify and analyze the first time that Jesus' prayer was answered, let's apply this same process to our time to get a better understanding of how Jesus' prayer will be answered in our time today. In looking at that first experience, we realize that it took place right after the devastating events of Jesus' crucifixion and the exhilarating events of His resurrection. We also discovered that historically there had been a number of governmental leaders, some good and some not so good, yet in spite of its checkered leadership, the conditions were favorable to the spread of the gospel. A fairly stable government, a common administrative system, Roman justice, an expanding citizenship, peace preserved by disciplined legions, roads pressing into every corner of the then-known world, and a language (Greek) that was almost universally understood were factors that favored the program undertaken by the apostles.

As we make the comparison to our day, even though things appear to be getting worse every week and we don't know how much longer these things will be true, we still have one of the most stable governments on the planet, an administrative process that is definable, an expanding citizenship, peace preserved by disciplined regions (for now), the ability to travel into every corner of the world, a language that is almost universally understood and the means to translate into any language in the world. So, for now, the conditions are present for Jesus' prayer to again be answered in our day and time.

In looking at the people who were involved in Jesus' prayer being answered the first time, we discovered that they did several critical things. It says that a certain group continued with one accord in prayer and supplication. They did not gather in the temple where they usually worshiped, but in the upper story of a private house, where they would be in seclusion, not in the general crowd but in a private prayer meeting with people that had a true, committed relationship with Christ. They also cooperated with heaven to choose a replacement for Judas, then remained obedient to the instruction of Jesus by staying in that upper room until they received the promise. And when the Day of Pentecost had fully come, these 120 people, plus other believers who may have joined them, were all with one accord in one place. And the Holy Ghost fell on them like cloven tongues of fire, and they were given the gift of tongues, and Peter preached, and 3,000 people were won to Christ. Then "they continued steadfastly in the apostles' doctrine and fellowship, in the breaking of bread, and in prayers. And fear came upon every soul, and they had all things in common, and they continuing daily with one accord in the temple, and breaking bread from house to house, they ate their food with gladness and simplicity of heart, praising God and having favor with all the people. And the Lord added to the church daily those who were being saved." And as we will show, all these conditions can be present in our day. So, now we see what the people were like that were involved in Jesus' prayer being answered the first time and how it can happen again.

In looking at what the Godhead did to facilitate Jesus' prayer being answered the first time, what we find still applies – God has still accepted His Son's sacrifice, and Jesus still sits on the right hand of His Father as our substitute and our advocate. And Joel 2:28–29 tells us that the Holy Spirit will do in our day what was done in that day. It says, "And it shall come to pass afterward that I will pour out My Spirit on all flesh; your sons and your daughters shall prophesy, your old men shall dream dreams, your young men shall see visions. And also, on My menservants and on My maidservants I will pour out My Spirit in those days."

So, we see that the times are comparable and that what the Godhead did then will be done again in our time. The only thing that needs to happen is for the people of God in this day to reproduce what the people of God in that day were doing.

❖ Continue with one accord in prayer and supplication,

❖ Not gather in the temple where they usually worshiped, but in the upper story of a private house, where they would be in seclusion, not in the general crowd but in a private prayer meeting with people that had a true, committed relationship with Christ

❖ Cooperate with heaven to choose our leaders in the church

❖ Remain obedient to the instruction of Jesus by staying in that upper room until they received the promise.

❖ Be in one accord in one place

❖ And then, maybe then, Joel 2 will be fulfilled, and the Holy Ghost will fall on us like cloven tongues of fire, and we will be given the gifts of the Spirit, and a Peter of our day, one who may have previously failed Jesus miserably but has been restored, will preach, and thousands will be won to Christ in a single day.

❖ And we must continue steadfastly in the apostles' doctrine and fellowship, in the breaking of bread, and in prayers. And a holy fear must come upon every soul (our Christianity has become too casual), and we must have all things in common, and continue daily with one accord as we worship Him, breaking bread from house to house, and we must learn to eat our food with gladness and simplicity of heart (not paying attention to titles or offices or degrees or social status or denominations), praising God and having favor with all the people. And then, maybe then, the Lord will add to the church (His church, the body of believers) daily those who desire to be saved. So, now that we see what factors were present when Jesus' prayer was answered the first time, I pray that we will understand what it will take for us to facilitate Jesus' prayer being answered in our day and time. Now, it's our turn. If we really love Jesus and want His prayer to be realized in us, let us take the steps just presented. May it become a reality amongst the people of God today. May we become one in Him.

What's Love Got To Do With It?

I n the previous chapter we received the assurance that Jesus' prayer will be answered in our day because it has already been answered before, during the time of the early church, when people of different backgrounds and ethnicities and understandings became one by studying and praying and worshiping and breaking bread together. And they remained in the gospel and in fellowship until they received the outpouring of Holy Ghost and were enabled to do marvelous things, and the church grew daily, and they remained one in Christ Jesus. Then, after reviewing the times and what the people and the Godhead were doing when Jesus' prayer was answered the first time, we realized that it can happen again in our time because the times are not much different, and the Godhead is the same, so the primary variable in Jesus' prayer being answered in our time is us, the people. What we need to do is reproduce what the people were doing in the time of the early church – study together, pray together, worship together, break bread together. Maybe then the promise of Joel 2 will take place. God will pour out His Spirit upon us and we will be able to do marvelous things, and the church without walls, without denominational labels, will grow into that special people (1 Peter 2:9 NKJV) that Jesus will be looking for when He returns the second time.

Now, having confirmed that Jesus' prayer will be answered again in our day, I would like to revisit a key point that was establish in the beginning of this chapter. As we anticipate God creating unity among His people in these last days, I suggest that we remind ourselves of what has always been the primary motivator of everything God does – love. In Chapter 4, entitled "The Original Plan and What Happened to It," we determined that creation was all about love, that from the very beginning the One who created all things, who has been described as the very embodiment of love in 1 John 4:8, put that love on display when He decided to create a world to house His most prized possession – mankind – and by how He created man.

So, because love is the primary motivator of everything God does, it is imperative that we recognize that love will once again be the primary motivator as God creates unity among believers in the last days. This is why this chapter is entitled, "What's Love Got To Do With It?" and my prayer is that by this discussion we as God's last day people will always be mindful of the fact that in all that we say and do, as we participate with God in preparing the world for the return of Jesus, love must be at its center. Love is the foundational glue that will hold God's people together in unity in these last days. Love must be for us what it is for God – the primary motivator behind all that we do. It is why Jesus established love as a primary focus for His disciples. In John 13:34–35 NKJV, He said "A new commandment I give to you, that you love one another; as I have loved you, that you also love one another. By this all will know that you are My disciples, if you have love for one another."

As members of the family of God, as we consider how we will participate in ensuring that Jesus' prayer will be answered in our day, let us be sure that we obey this commandment and have love for all who are or will soon be a part of the family. This is also emphasized in 1 John 4:7 NKJV, "Beloved, let us love one another, for love is of God; and everyone who loves is born of God and knows God." It is not the name that we call ourselves or place where we worship or the works that we do that qualifies us to be a part of the family of God. John tells us that everyone who loves is born of God, making them a child of God that possess a love that shows everyone who they are. It is love that will restore the reputation of Christianity. It is love that will draw people to Christ. And it is love that will make us one in Him. Now we are seeing what's love got to do with it.

It is here that the Holy Spirit led me to understand how love equips us to share the truth as it is found in God's Word. A core element of Christianity is knowing and sharing God's truth, and to experience the joy and privilege of taking the light of God's truth to the world. And as we seek to be good neighbors in the community of believers and participate in drawing others to Christ, it is of utmost importance that we make sure that people don't just know how much we know, but that they also know how much we love and care for them. As we reproduce the environment of the early church – when Jesus' prayer for unity was answered the first time – and we facilitate growth in the community of believers by studying together and praying together and worshiping together and breaking bread together, and we settle all differences and remove all the things that separate us and become one in Christ Jesus, it is then that the Joel 2 experience happens among the community of believers. It is then that we will receive the Holy Ghost and receive the gifts and power of the Spirit to fulfill the great commission to take the full, untainted gospel truth to the world.

In Ephesians 4:13–16, we see how the gifts of the Holy Spirit and unity and truth and love all combine to make the community of believers the powerful force that will prepare the world for the coming of Jesus. The scripture says, "Till we all come to the unity of the faith and of the knowledge of the Son of God, to a perfect man, to the measure of the stature of the fullness of Christ; that we should no longer be children, tossed to and fro and carried about with every wind of doctrine, by the trickery of men, in the cunning craftiness of deceitful plotting, but, speaking the truth in love, may grow up in all things into Him who is the head—Christ, from whom the whole body, joined and knit together by what every joint supplies, according to the effective working by which every part does it share, causes growth of the body for the edifying of itself in love."

Let's look at what this text is saying. It is telling us that it is not until we come together in the unity of the faith and the knowledge of Jesus Christ that we will measure up to the full and complete standard of Jesus Christ. So, you see that this divided state we are currently in does not allow us, individually or collectively, to measure up the standard of Jesus. The text also says, that by coming together in the unity of the faith and knowledge of Jesus Christ, the community of believers will no longer be immature like children, tossed and blown about by every wind of new teaching and false doctrine, and will not be tricked or try to trick others with lies so clever that they sound like the truth. That is why it is so important that we operate as a community of believers, for it keeps the truth of God front and center and prevents false doctrines and misinformation and misinterpretations of the truth from dividing us.

Ephesians 4:15 brings two key ingredients together – truth and love. It says that instead of God's people being like immature children who are tossed and blown about by fake truths and fake news, we who know the truth will, by the Spirit of God and the love of God being in us, speak the truth in love, and that both us as the speakers and those who are the hearers will grow in every way more and more like the head of the church, Jesus Christ. This allows verse 16 to be our reality, with each part doing its own special work, helping the other parts grow, so that the whole body is healthy and growing and full of love. Do you see how this all comes together? When the people of God allow the Holy Spirit to be in control, it is possible for unity and truth and love to lead to a growing, vibrant community of believers. Yes, now we are seeing what's love got to do with it.

And the amazing part is that we, as fallen mankind, have the privilege of not only enjoying the love of God but also being considered sons and daughters of the God. 1 John 3:1 NKJV says, "Behold what manner of love the Father has bestowed on us, that we should be called children of God! Therefore, the world does not know us, because it did not know Him." As sons and daughters of God, we must make sure that we are presenting God's truth in love so that those who we are being drawn to Christ will realize the fullness of the love that God the Father wants to bestow upon them as His children. The problem that many who don't know God is having is that some who call themselves Christians are not telling the truth in love. It is a necessity that we as the people of God tell the truth in love because many people today are operating based on a truth that is not true or that is not based on love. They are living according to a truth based mainly on what they perceive and want to believe. We must understand that when an individual settles on a truth, it affects all their senses: what they see, what they hear (or don't hear), what they smell, how they taste, and how they feel. It was here that the Holy Spirit showed me that we as Christians should be careful how we judge others because we do some of the same things they do.

We must understand that anytime anyone, ourselves included, operates by a truth that is not of God, when we establish a truth based on how we feel or what we perceive or what we want to believe, that it affects all our senses, determines how we treat others, and how we respond to life. We saw this on January 6, 2021, when the very seat of our democracy became the site of clashing passions and the unthinkable was done. And what was most alarming about that event was that there were many there who called themselves Christians, which makes one wonder how that could be. But as we consider the division that exists among believers both historically and presently, as we consider how we think about one another and how we talk about one another and how we treat one another, we might realize that it is not a problem just with supporters of Donald Trump or Black Lives Matter or antiabortionists or freedom of choice advocates, but it could also exist between Adventists and Catholics and Baptists and Methodists.

At the root of all division and dissention and separation, and what drives us to do the unthinkable to one another, is the absence of the pure, untainted truth of God being spoken in love. It was the absence of truth and love that led Cain to kill his brother Abel. It was the absence of truth and love that led David to kill Uriah. It was the absence of truth and love that led the leaders of the church to kill the very Son of God, and it is the absence of truth and love that leads to all the unrest we see in the church and the world today. Yes, now we see what love's got to do with it.

So, now the question is, "What are we going to do about it?" To answer this question, let's once again go back to the time of Jesus and look at what brought about change. As we look at what Jesus did, let's consider another question that will help us determine what we need to do today. That question is: What kind of people do you pull together when you're trying to change the world? What kind of mission and focus do you give that will draw them together, keep them together, make them work together even when they are imperfect, have an improper focus or may even be looking out for themselves? Jesus was attempting to replace a culture that had been developed over hundreds of years, one that was not good for mankind. My brothers and sisters, whether we realize it or not, this is what we have been called to do – in homes, neighborhoods, jobs, even in our churches—to replace a culture that has been developed over hundreds of years, one that is not of God. And we are to do it with the culture spoken of in Ephesians 4:16, where the whole body is joined and knit together, with each part doing its own special work, helping the other parts grow, so that the whole body is healthy and growing and full of love. This is what Jesus called the kingdom of God and is what He introduced to the world. So, let's determine how Jesus sought to accomplish this culture change by considering the primary agents that were called to implement it, the twelve disciples:

- ❖ Peter – foot-shaped mouth; impetuous; reactive

- ❖ Andrew – had an amazing ability to see the value of small, modest things, individual people (he didn't baptize 3K but did bring Peter to the Lord), brought the lad with the five loaves and two fish; was often hidden in the background

❖ James – one of the sons of thunder; hot tempered; manipulative (put his mother up to appeal to Jesus for a seat of honor)

❖ John – the other son of thunder; brother of James; zealous, passionate, fervent; shows us what should happen as we grow in Christ, allowing the Lord's strength to be made perfect in our weakness

❖ Philip – the bean counter; pessimistic, pragmatic, cynical

❖ Nathaniel – the guileless one; 'can any good thing come out of Nazareth'; judgmental; arrogant

❖ Matthew – tax collector; dishonest by trade; considered a despicable scoundrel

❖ Thomas – doubter; pessimistic;

❖ James – the less; may have been small in stature or younger than the others, a quite person

❖ Simon – the zealot; probably a former member of a Zealots political party (a feared outlaw group); may have been a partner of Judas Iscariot; may have had similar political reasons to follow Jesus initially, but Simon actually accepted Jesus and became a true believer, Judas never did

❖ Judas (not Iscariot) – meek; minor player (John 14:21, 22)

❖ Judas Iscariot – the traitor

With all their faults and character flaws, as remarkably ordinary as they were, these men carried on a ministry after Jesus' ascension that left an indelible impact on the world forever, with their ministry continuing to influence us even today. God graciously empowered and used these men to inaugurate the spread of the gospel message and to turn the world upside down (Acts 17:6). Ordinary men, people like you and me, became the instruments by which Christ's message was carried to the ends of the then known world. So, as we consider who Jesus used to change the culture of that day and turn the world upside down, we must recognize that He can do the same with us today.

Just like with the disciples, it was not about who we are at the moment but what we become in Christ Jesus. Just like them, we may have trouble loving ourselves in our present condition, but we must not look to ourselves, but look unto Jesus, the author and finisher of our faith (Hebrews 12:2). Like the disciples, we must follow the orders of Jesus as shown in John 13:34–35 NLT "So now I am giving you a new commandment: Love each other. Just as I have loved you, you should love each other. Your love for one another will prove to the world that you are my disciples." How did the disciples turn the world upside down? They did it by making love their mission, by realizing that love was the answer. Love must come from the right source. Jesus' love was not environmentally based. It was not based on what was going on around Him. It did not change based on external influences. Jesus' love came, and our love must come, from above.

There is a lot of talk about tough love. Well, the Holy Spirit showed me what tough love really is. Tough love is love that is tough enough to withstand whatever is done to it. Tough love is love that allows you to ignore how you're treated, what is said about you, or what is done to you. In the face of the worse treatment (even death), it does not change. Tough love is love that allows you to withstand being misunderstood and mis-represented. Tough love is love that does not seek attention. It is love that posts on Facebook, not to draw attention to oneself but to bring glory and honor to God and to edify (make better) God's people. Tough love is love that responds gracefully and intensely to false love, whose response is not based on how false love affects me or makes me feel but engenders a response based on what is best for the false lover, whatever will alert them to their true condition and help them experience true love.

We may even be asked to show the kind of love that Jesus showed in the story of Lazarus, a love that seeks to glorify God even if it makes you look bad in the moment, like you don't care, that may temporarily damage your reputation. Attempts may even be made to capitalize on this kind of love by those who don't understand what you are doing, like the other mourners in that story. "He didn't really love you anyway.

Look, we were here first, we're here now, have even been sitting with you for three days. Where is He? He hasn't shown up yet." And when Jesus did show up, He not only showed what real love looks like, but He also showed the power of God's love. We may be asked to show that kind of love.

Let's remember the kind of love 1 Corinthians 13 instructs us to have: love that is patient and kind, love that is not jealous or boastful or proud or rude, that does not demand its own way, that is not irritable, that keeps no record of being wronged, that does not rejoice about injustice but rejoices whenever the truth wins out, a love that never gives up, never loses faith, is always hopeful, and endures through every circumstance. Yes, we need to have a tough love, a love that is tough to have, tough to live, tough to be consistent with, but tough enough to withstand any and everything, that makes us tough the Jesus way, that places the mind and heart in us that was also in Christ Jesus (Philippians 2:5–8).

As we close this chapter, some of us may be wondering how God is going to get us to the place where we can change the current culture and turn our world upside down in this present time. I ask you to consider the story of an old harpist who, as he tunes his harp, strikes the strings, and finding them way out of tune, he pulls the strings, stretching them to what seems like the breaking point. Then he strikes them again, listening for the right sound. He wants each string to have a desired pitch until it plays a melodious chord. My brothers and sisters, the tests and trials and challenges of life is God's way of striking the strings to see what sound we will make, and He will keep stretching us and testing us until the sound of His love rings sure and true and creates the beautiful music of the gospel that will draw all men unto Him. And listen, He knows what He is doing!!!

We become tunable as we surrender to God, and are therefore well-tuned when we reach the point where we receive the mind, attitude and heart of Jesus and can say what He said in Luke 22:42 NLT – "Father, if you are willing, please take this cup of suffering away from me (don't strike my strings this way; don't pull them this hard). Yet I want your will to be done, not mine." Do whatever you think is necessary to get me in tune, so that the sound of love will permeate everything I do and say, so that it will help me love those that right now seem hard for me to love, so that the beauty of your gospel truth will sound like music to all those around me, so that they will be drawn to You, Oh God.

WHAT'S LOVE GOT TO DO WITH IT...EVERY-THING!!! Love is that powerful Counterforce that preexisted the divisive force of the enemy. Love is the force that rules the cosmos, yea even created it. Love is the force in operation on the spokes on that old wagon wheel, that draws everyone to the hub, aka Christ Jesus, as they respond to the loving call of God. And as we are drawn to the Christ, we are drawn closer together until we meet in the middle and become one in Him. So, if anyone asks you WHAT'S LOVE GOT TO DO WITH IT...you tell them EVERYTHING!!! It's all about love.

Evidence

As we have progressed along this journey on how to be one in Christ, I have come to the realization that God really does have a plan in place to gather together His own special people, especially after what we have reviewed in the last few chapters. After receiving a better understanding of what comprises the community of believers, realizing the essence of the real Lord's prayer, celebrating that Jesus' prayer will be answered in our day, and recognizing how love, being the eternal force that powers every act of God and will power the creation of the community of believers in these last days, I now have confidence that this thing will happen. In spite of how things look now, this journey has helped me believe that it will happen, and also to understand how God's people can and will be one in Christ Jesus. I pray that it has had the same effect on you and all other believers that will read these pages. Now that these truths have been revealed, let's consider how we will know that it is happening once again in our day. Let's look at the "Evidence."

As was established in Chapter 10, the primary reason we can be so confident that Jesus' prayer for all believers to be one in Him will be answered in our day is because it has already happened before. And while there may be many different types of evidence that indicate that Jesus' prayer is being answered, in this chapter we will focus on one thing in particular that stands out as irrefutable evidence, and that is when people who were once deeply divided come together as one.

As we determined early in this journey, division and disunity is what Satan brought from heaven to earth to disrupt God's creation and separate man from God and from each other.

So, a critical piece of evidence that Jesus' prayer is being answered is when the attempts of the enemy to divide are overruled, unity reigns in its stead, and people become one. Ephesians 2:13–14 NKJV describes it this way, "But now in Christ Jesus you who once were far off have been brought near by the blood of Christ. For He Himself is our peace, who has made both one, and has broken down the middle wall of separation."

In the context of this chapter, we will consider the fulfillment of this evidence by reviewing both the early church at the time of Pentecost and the Great Awakening in the 1800s at the time of the advent movement. Both of these times were marked by a group of people that came together to understand the truth of God. And it was the untainted truth, coupled with their intense desire to not only understand God's truth but to live by it, that brought about a result that yielded evidence that something special was happening. By reviewing the evidence of Jesus' prayer being answered in those times we hope to see what evidence we can look for that will show God's people of today that Jesus' prayer is being answered in our time. As we do this review, we will also look at Biblical references that indicate that God has always done what we have been studying about and are looking forward to, that He is well able to take people that were once divided and bring them together for His purposes.

As we consider these two examples, the first piece of evidence we find is that the believers in both those instances did come together. In Acts 1:14 it says that the disciples, the mother and brothers of Jesus, and the other women who followed and supported Jesus in His ministry, all came together, about 120 of them, and the scripture states, "These all continued with one accord in prayer and supplication." And after they had received the promise of the Holy Spirit and Peter had preached, adding about 3,000 souls to the body of believers, Acts 2:42, 44 NKJV reads, "And they continued steadfastly in the apostles' doctrine and fellowship, in the breaking of bread and in prayers. Now all who believed were together and had all things in common."

Then, we also learned that the advent movement was pioneered by a Baptist minister named William Miller. Miller, who with other advent members from various mainline Protestant denominations, began reading the prophecies of

Daniel and the Revelation, including the prophecies of Revelation Chapter 14. And as a result of their studies together, the subsequent great disappointment, and their continued studies that clarified their error, these people who were once not a people became a people. In his book "Grace On Trial," Robert Wieland stated that it was from this understanding of prophecy that the name "Adventist" was born, identifying a people who believes that Christ's second coming is near. More than that, the name means one who loves the thought that it is near.

The Seventh-day Adventist Church sprang from a phenomenal conviction in the hearts of some humble Christians from different denominations that came together and discovered in the Bible a prophetic road map. Of this group, Wieland writes "Their hearts were in union with Christ. Because they sensed some appreciation for His character of love, they wanted Him to return. For that group of Christians of many different churches, there was no self-centered motivation to cloud the bright flame of their devotion to Christ. They became one in Him." And we can be sure that there are many other examples of diverse groups of people being brought into unity by the study of God's Word. I love the way 1 Peter 2:10 describes this phenomenon. It proclaims these are people "who once *were* not a people but *are* now the people of God."

So, as we look for evidence in our day of whether Jesus' prayer is being answered, whether believers are becoming one in Him, we must simply look for groups of believers that were once not a people coming together and becoming a people. And praise God, I am seeing just that. I don't know about you, but I have been experiencing this personally over the last ten plus years and it has had a profound effect on me. I would even say that it was these experiences that led to this book.

Over these last few years God has provided opportunities for me to fellowship with a number of believers from other denominations, to build wonderful relationships with them and to see how much they also love the Lord. I've been blessed to participate in an international organization named Nehemiah Project International Ministries, made up of Christian entrepreneurs whose mission is to establish kingdom business and spread the gospel of Jesus in the marketplace. I was led to become a certified instructor and business coach for them, teaching and guiding believers on how to establish kingdom businesses. I serve on the board of a ministry called Teach 'Em to Fish, a wonderful group of ministers and laypersons from different churches that are engaged in community development through entrepreneurship and employee training and job creation.

In addition, I participate in a men's prayer line that meets Monday through Friday that is made up of men of several different denominations. This group has formed an amazingly tight bond as we prayer together, visit each other's churches and worship together, visit each other's homes and fellowship together, and have additional Bible studies together outside of the prayer line. Pastors from different denominations speak on this prayer line. We respect each other's present Christian experience as we grow together. And on every Friday, we wish each other a rich worship experience on our chosen day of worship.

In all these experiences, there may be times, either covertly or overtly, of hesitancy and unsureness about each other, times when our beliefs collided, and we have had to work things out. But over time, as we studied together and prayed together and worked together, we grew closer together, the hesitancy and unsureness were replaced with relationship. And as a result of the relationships that were formed, the victories and answered prayers that we are experiencing together, and how the truth of God was being embraced together, I have evidence that Jesus' prayer is being answered in our day.

It is happening now my brothers and sisters, and I am sure that there are many other examples of believers coming together around the world. And my prayer for us all is that we will start looking for this evidence, taking advantage of opportunities to interact with and build relationships with others in the community of believers, that we will share with each other the truth received from the Lord in love, recognizing that God is speaking to all His children. And it is in this kind of fellowship that what happened in the early church and what happened in the advent movement will happen again in our day, that the community of believers will grow together, and those that at one time were not a people will become the people of God.

I found several texts in the Old Testament that provided references to this phenomenon of believers coming together.

Isaiah 11:12–13 NKJV reads, "He will set up a banner for the nations, and will assemble the outcasts of Israel, and gather together the dispersed of Judah from the four corners of the earth. Also, the envy of Ephraim shall depart, And the adversaries of Judah shall be cut off; Ephraim shall not envy Judah, And Judah shall not harass Ephraim." The SDA Commentaries says, that in principle, this promise is to be fulfilled to spiritual Israel, the church. Accordingly, these words point to the great work of deliverance from sin now going on in every part of the world. Everywhere men and women are acting as ensigns, or beacons, for heaven, guiding men and women into the way of light and truth. The work now being witnessed is in fulfillment of Isaiah's prophecy and is an earnest example of great things yet to come.

It also says, regarding the envy of Ephraim departing, that the history of the people of God was a history of jealousy, envy, trouble, dissension and war. Isaiah's vision of the future would not be perfect or complete if it did not envision a healing of the old wounds and a reconciliation between Israel and Judah. And I believe that in the context of our day, this promise points to a healing and a reconciliation between members in the community of believers. For too long, we have been looking at each other suspiciously. For too long, we have been focusing on our differences. It is time for us to now follow God's lead as He sets up a banner for the nations, and assembles the outcasts of Israel, and gather together the dispersed of Judah from the four corners of the earth. Now is the time for the people of God to become one in Him.

The Holy Spirit also led me to Isaiah 52:8 which proclaims, "Your watchmen shall lift up their voices, with their voices they shall sing together; For they shall see eye to eye when the LORD brings back Zion." Look at Jeremiah 3:18, "In those days the house of Judah shall walk with the house of Israel, and they shall come together out of the land of the north to the land that I have given as an inheritance to your fathers." Jeremiah 50:4 further states, "In those days and in that time," says, the LORD, "The children of Israel shall come, They and the children of Judah together; With continual weeping they shall come, and seek the LORD their God." Hosea 1:11 reads, "Then the children of Judah and the children of Israel shall be gathered together, and appoint for themselves one head; and they shall come up out of the land, for great will be the day of Jezreel!" And then Zephaniah 3:9 reports, "For then I will restore to the peoples a pure language, that they all may call on the name of the LORD, to serve Him with one accord."

It was these Old Testament references that led me to recognize the beauty of this evidence, and it gave more meaning to the New Testament description of this evidence, when the community of believers are all finally gathered together into one fold. John 10:14–16 says, "I am the good shepherd; and I know My *sheep*, and am known by My own. As the Father knows Me, even so I know the Father; and I lay down My life for the sheep. And other sheep I have which are not of this fold; them also I must bring, and they will hear My voice; and there will be one flock *and* one shepherd." And Ephesians 2:14–18 describes it this way, "For He Himself is our peace, who has made both one, and has broken down the middle wall of separation, having abolished in His flesh the enmity, that is, the law of commandments contained in ordinances, so as to create in Himself one new man from the two, thus making peace, and that He might reconcile them both to God in one body through the cross, thereby putting to death the enmity. And He came and preached peace to you who were afar off and to those who were near. For through Him we both have access by one Spirit to the Father."

Listen family, the evidence is clear. God has done it in the past and He intends to do it again. He will bring His people together and we must not, in our blindness, miss seeing the evidence. There is a deep necessity for believers to stop relying on their own assessments and understanding. We cannot trust ourselves. When a situation arises or people do something that impacts us in a negative way, instead of responding or reacting based on our thoughts and opinions, we should ask God through Holy Spirit to tell us how to think about things, knowing that He is all about bringing His people together, not dividing us. We must respond to the situations of life based on Holy Spirit direction. It is then that we will be living not according to the flesh but according to the Spirit. It is then that dying to self will be our daily reality and we will be able to become one in Christ Jesus with all believers, just as Jesus prayed for. It is when the people of God are, as a community of believers, being led by the same Holy Spirit, as we rely less and less on our own perceptions and perspectives and more and more on Holy Spirit guidance, that the gap between us grows smaller and smaller as we move closer to Jesus and being one in Him becomes a reality.

As I studied this, I realized that the thinking of some believers will have to be retrained. I was reminded of a story told to me by a friend on the men's prayer line. Before he became a Seventh-day Adventist Christian, he was in the military and was assigned to become a marksman, an expert in shooting whatever gun they gave him. He said that he grew up never shooting a gun, and he was placed in a unit with men that had been shooting guns all their lives. His sergeant told him not to worry, that if he listened to him, he would become a skilled marksman. The men who had been shooting all their lives had a more difficult time because they had to unlearn what they had been taught, and my friend became an expert because he had no previous knowledge that needed to be unlearned. I believe this same principle was applied by Jesus. This is why Jesus didn't go to the church to find His disciples. He chose men that had no affiliation with the church. It is possible that Jesus didn't want to have to deal with people that needed to unlearn stuff before they learn the true gospel from Him. We may have to unlearn some things before we can rightly share the gospel of Jesus Christ.

We must retrain our thinking and learn not to consider His truth as our possession, and to receive the light from above as a gift from our loving Father to be shared with the community of believers. And it is the sharing of these glorious fractions of light, combining and studying them together, allowing the Holy Spirit to hover over the marvelous laboratory of loving Christian brotherhood, as He did during Creation, and proclaiming "Let there be light," that the shared light will become a glorious beacon. "The prophetic word confirmed, which you do well to heed as a light that shines in a dark place, until the day dawns and the morning star rises in your hearts" (2 Peter 1:19 NKJV)

My brothers and sisters, let the Word of God be the platform for unity, not the foundation for division. Let us begin all theological discussion with the end in mind, that we become one in Him, so that the world may believe by our unity that He, the Word made flesh, was sent by God (John 17:21). It is then that the glory which God gave His son will be given to and seen in us, the worldwide family of God, and the whole world will see the evidence that we are His own special people and will want to join the family of God, being one in Christ Jesus.

All Are Invited!!!

As we have proceeded through this journey, God through His Spirit has revealed so much to us – about Himself, about ourselves, and about His desires for us as His children. In the previous chapter we reviewed the evidence and determined that it is clear, God has in the past, and will again in our day, position His people to be the answer to Jesus' prayer and become one in Him. Now we will establish a very important fact about Jesus' prayer that all God's children must also be clear on. That fact is made clear by the title of this chapter – "All Are Invited."

Throughout this study, we have acknowledged the reality that mankind, and Christianity, is very divided right now, and it seems like it is getting worse instead of better. As we watch the news and see all that is happening around us, it appears that the gap that divides us is growing wider and wider, the reasons for being divided are ever increasing, and hatred among people is becoming more prevalent. But what we, the body of believers, must also recognize is that this did not catch

God by surprise. God, through His Son Jesus, not only warned us of this but also told us what we should do when these times came upon us. In Matthew 24:12–14 Jesus said, "¹²And because lawlessness will abound, the love of many will grow cold. ¹³ But he who endures to the end shall be saved. ¹⁴ And this gospel of the kingdom will be preached in all the world as a witness to all the nations, and then the end will come."

In other words, what Jesus is telling us is that even though times may get crazy, and people will start hating one another, if we who know and love the truth of God hang in there and stay with Jesus, we will be saved. But Jesus' admonition does not end there. He ends by saying it is in this crazy environment that we must spread the gospel to the whole world, and that we must do it as a witness. That means getting into the mix, being among people, showing them what it means and what it looks like to be a child of God, sharing the truth in love, letting everyone know that all are invited to become a part of God's family. And the scripture says, that when we have done this, when everyone has heard about the Savior and how He has died for all, when everyone has received their invitation to join the family of God, then the end would come. It is widely accepted among theologians that when Jesus made this statement, He was replying to the disciples' questions about the end times, and He blended in His answer regarding events leading up to the end of the Jewish nation as God's chosen people, and "the end" of the world, the last days, our time. So, it is important that we take heed to what Jesus is saying and take seriously our assignment to be a witness in the world today.

So, the question is, how are we supposed to fulfill our role of being a witness and distributors of the gospel in this kind of environment? Zechariah provides a vital perspective as we seek to answer that question. To understand the setting in which this perspective was given, the SDA Commentaries tells us that Zechariah was a contemporary of Haggai and was appointed by God to arouse to action the Jews who, because of enemy opposition, had left off the building of the Temple. Zechariah's prophecies came at a time of great uncertainty and anxiety, when it seemed to the leaders as if the permission granted the Jews to rebuild the temple was about to be withdrawn. His message, dealing with the work of God and the divine plans for the restoration, was designed to bring encouragement to the weakening zeal of the Jews. And as a result of the inspiring messages and leadership of Haggai and Zechariah, the Temple was soon completed.

In comparison, we find that this perspective is vital to us today. Many modern-day believers are intimidated by all that is happening around us. Opposition to the cause of Christ appears to be great and there is much uncertainty and anxiety. Some may wonder if we can really spread the gospel in this environment. But just as it did for the Jews of that time, Zechariah's message is to be reflected on and embraced, so that it can bring encouragement to the weakening zeal of God's people today. Zechariah's testimony in Chapter 4:2–6 reads, "And he said to me, 'What do you see?' So I said, "I am looking, and there *is* a lampstand of solid gold with a bowl on top of it, and on the *stand* seven lamps with seven pipes to the seven lamps. Two olive trees *are* by it, one at the right of the bowl and the other at its left." So I answered and spoke to the angel who talked with me, saying, "What are these, my lord?" Then the angel who talked with me answered and said to me, "Do you not know what these are?" And I said, "No, my lord." So, he answered and said to me: "This *is* the word of the Lord to Zerubbabel: 'Not by might nor by power, but by My Spirit,' says, the Lord of hosts."

So, what does all this mean and how does it provide encouragement for us today as we seek to be a witness in this environment, to make sure that we complete the task of letting everyone know that all are invited to be a part of the family of God? Here is the explanation: the lampstand, the bowl, the pipes, the two olive trees all represent how God will supply His people with heavenly guidance. Oh, that's enough to give us confidence right there!

According to verse 14 of this chapter, the two olive trees are the two anointed ones that stand beside the Lord of the whole earth. The commentaries explain that oil furnished by the olive trees represents the Holy Spirit; divine grace alone could overcome all the obstacles that confronted God's people during those times and during our time today. It also says the two olive trees, also mentioned by John, the revelator, in Revelation 11:4, where he parallels them with "The two candlesticks standing before the God of the earth," represent the scriptures of the Old and the New Testament, which Psalm

119:105 says, "Is a lamp unto my feet, and a light unto my path." These two anointed ones represent the heavenly instrumentalities through which the Holy Spirit is imparted to human beings who are wholly consecrated to God's service. "The mission of the two anointed ones is to communicate light and power to God's people" (Testimonies to Ministers and Gospel Workers p. 510).

Those who receive such a heavenly imparting are expected, in turn, to communicate these blessings to others, **but only with the aid of heavenly support.** So, there you have it. This is the key to Zechariah's instruction to the Jews of his day, and to us in this day. The only way we will be able to accomplish this end time assignment is only with the assistance of the Aide of Heaven. That is how we are supposed to fulfill our role as distributors of the gospel in this kind of environment. Only with Holy Ghost power as received by studying God's Holy Word! We must have the Holy Spirit and the Word within us. And how will we get the power to do that great work? GOD WILL PROVIDE IT!!! And like Peter on the day of Pentecost, we will be able to extend the invitation to all people with great power, regardless of their background or ethnicity or social status or beliefs, to come and be a part of the family of God.

But I am reminded here what will also make our witness so effective. The presence of the Holy Spirit will not only provide power, but it will also yield fruit. Because of the presence of the fruit of the Spirit, our very nature will be so profoundly changed that we will not only extend this invitation to all people with great power but it will be done in such a manner that it will compel them to accept the invitation. Imagine the impact God's people would have if we went into the world with the fruit of the Spirit in full display—love, joy, peace, patience, kindness, goodness, faithfulness, gentleness, and self-control. As we have discussed previously, it is in this context that Joel 2:28-29 will come into full effect. "And it shall come to pass afterward that I will pour out My Spirit on all flesh; your sons and your daughters shall prophesy, your old men shall dream dreams, your young men shall see visions. And also, on *My* menservants and on *My* maidservants I will pour out My Spirit in those days."

Let's dissect this scripture more thoroughly to understand what is being offered to us. The SDA Commentaries, Vol. 4 p. 946, says that the phrase 'afterward' is indefinite as to time. It was God's plan to bestow upon the restored state of Israel the spiritual blessings described in this verse. But because of the failure of the people, and the consequent rejection of the Jewish nation, the promises were not fulfilled to literal Israel. So, guess what? These promises were therefore transferred to spiritual Israel...you and me!!! We now have the promise of receiving this outpouring. Also note that Peter, in his sermon on the day of Pentecost, identified the partial fulfillment of this Joel prophecy, but instead of saying 'afterward,' Peter used the phrase 'in the last days.' Joel prophesied that God's Spirit will be poured out "upon all flesh," those of various age groups (old and young), those that are free and in the family of God (sons and daughters), and those that are still slaves and not yet formally in the family (manservants and maidservants).

It was here that I was led to understand a marvelous truth, and it was shown to me in both an Old Testament and a New Testament context. The text in Joel presents this marvelous truth in the Old Testament context, that all are invited to receive this outpouring of the Holy Spirit – sons, daughters, old, young, even on the male and female servants (those not officially in the family). Yes, all are invited to be a part of this outpouring, to receive Holy Ghost power and to participate in this last day effort to spread the gospel of Jesus Christ.

Praise God, I was also shown this marvelous truth in the New Testament context, found in Hebrews 8:7–12 NKJV, (which actually has an Old Testament link to Jeremiah 31). It speaks of the new covenant that God has established with His people. The scripture says, "For if that first *covenant* had been faultless, then no place would have been sought for a second. Because finding fault with them, He says: "Behold, the days are coming, says, the Lord, when I will make a new covenant with the house of Israel and with the house of Judah." (Note that whenever we see a reference to the house of Israel and the house of Judah, it means that it is for spiritual Israel, the body of believers, the Christian church who is the inheritor of the spiritual privileges and responsibilities that once belonged to literal Israel; so God is saying 'I will make a new covenant with you, the body of believers that Jesus prayed for in John 17). "Not according to the covenant that I made with their fathers in the day when I took them by the hand to lead them out of the land of Egypt; because they did not continue in My covenant, and I disregarded them, says, the Lord." The eighth chapter of Hebrews presents the fact that by the eternal priesthood of Christ the Levitical priesthood of Aaron is abolished. And it also presents the critical fact that the temporal covenant made with the fathers (the children of Israel in their desert journey from Egypt) is replaced by the eternal/everlasting covenant of the gospel.

It was what the Holy Spirit showed me about the everlasting covenant in Hebrews 8:7–12, combined with the prophecy about God pouring out His Spirit in the last days in Joel 2, that helped me to understand how we are to accomplish getting the invitation out to everyone. Verse 10 says, "For this *is* the covenant that I will make with the house of Israel after those days, says, the Lord: I will put My laws in their mind and write them on their hearts; and I will be their God, and they shall be My people." Check out the key elements of this new covenant:

❖ I will put My laws in their mind and write them on their hearts – at Mt. Sinai the Lord wrote His laws on tables of stone. He intended that these laws should also be written on the hearts of the people. But the Israelites were content to regard these statutes simply as an external code, and their observance to them as a matter of outward compliance. This is not what God intended. He offered His people the experience of a new heart. Ezekiel 36:26–27 says "I will give you a new heart and put a new spirit within you; I will take the heart of stone out of your flesh and give you a heart of flesh. [27] I will put My Spirit within you and cause you to walk in My statutes, and you will keep My judgments and do *them*." But they were content with only an external religion (WARNING: we must be careful not to make the same mistake of having an external religion that focuses on outward compliance instead of an inward presence of the Spirit of God in our hearts).

❖ Under the new covenant men's hearts and minds are changed, and they do right, not by their own will power and strength, but because Christ dwells in their heart, they live out His life, and they are born of the Spirit and bear the fruits of the Spirit (love, joy, peace, patience, kindness, goodness, faithfulness, gentleness, self-control). Living according to the old covenant, focusing on compliance and law-keeping, does not give you these traits. Only living under the new covenant, receiving God's law and love in our hearts can do that.

❖ Then God will be our God, and we will be His people.

Then, Hebrews 8:11 says, "None of them shall teach his neighbor, and none his brother, saying, 'Know the Lord,' for all shall know Me, from the least of them to the greatest of them." Now we come to the meat of this chapter's focus. Verse 11 presents some critical information about how the new covenant will be realized in the last days.

❖ 'None of them shall teach his neighbor, and none his brother, saying 'Know the Lord,' the SDA Commentaries Vol. 7 p. 446 says, that in the last days, when the prophecy of Joel 2:28–29 is being experienced, and the Spirit of God is being poured out upon all flesh, that there would be no need of continual admonition and counsel, no need for constant and persistent reprimand and rebuke and scolding, for all who are earnestly seeking God and are open to receiving Him will have a personal religious experience, a personal encounter with God ("And you will seek Me and find Me, when you search for Me with all your heart" Jeremiah 29:13 NKJV). They will have an individual experience with the Holy Spirit because he is being poured out upon all flesh. Then those who know and receive the Lord as their Savior can have direct access to God without an intermediary, a go-between. They won't need to depend on a priest or wait on a pastor to know the ways of God, for the rest of verse 11 says, "For all shall know Me, from the least of them to the greatest of them."

❖ The key question I asked the Holy Spirit here was, "Who is 'them' in Hebrews 8:11, the least of them, the greatest of them? "Could the least of them be those that we don't think so highly of, those that don't look like us or worship like us or live like us, those that are addicted or homeless or live in the projects? Could the greatest of them be the rich and famous, congressmen and senators on Capitol Hill, those that sit in the penthouse or the White House? I believe that 'them' includes all of the above. They all will know the Lord, will have a personal religious experience, a personal encounter with God, and an individual experience with the Holy Spirit because they are earnestly seeking Him, open to receiving Him and what is being poured out upon all flesh. …the least of them (DMX)…the greatest of them (Donald Trump). All who position themselves properly with God in these last days will receive His Spirit, shall know Him, and they all will be invited to be a part of the family of God and become one in Him.

Verse 12 of Hebrews 8 says, "For I will be merciful to their unrighteousness, and their sins and their lawless deeds I will remember no more." HALLELUJAH!!! For the believer, for the one that looks to God and trusts in Him, these words are a promise of forgiveness full and free through the blood of Jesus, without the shedding of blood of animals as under the old Levitical system. God will be merciful and forgive, and their sins and lawless deeds He will remember no more; that is, God will no longer hold these sins against the transgressor; He will cast all our sins behind His back (Isa. 38:17) into the depth of the sea (Micah 7:19)!!! I am reminded of the promise found in 2 Peter 3:9, "The Lord is not slack concerning His promise, as some count slackness, but is longsuffering toward us, not willing that **any** should perish but that **all** (all flesh, all that will receive the outpouring of the Holy Spirit, all that will know Him from the least to the greatest) should come to repentance," and be saved in His kingdom. That is why all must be invited!!

So, as we prepare to finish this great work of the gospel, let us remember the **_inclusiveness_** of this new covenant and the inclusiveness of this invitation. It is not for us to choose who we think should receive it. It is not based on who we are comfortable with, whether their looks meet our criteria, or their speech includes words that agree with us or sound like us. It is not for us to determine who should receive the outpouring of the Spirit. It is not for us to determine who we think knows the Lord, who the least of them or the greatest of them are. Some may not even be participating in organized religion, which may be God's will, because organized religion as they have encountered it was not according to His will. The main point is this – we must take the gospel to all our world, invite everyone that God brings into our path, and don't underestimate the presence of God in others. Hebrews 8:11 says, "All will know Him." Some may just need us to help them understand the meaning of that yearning that they have in their hearts.

The key for us is surrender. The outpouring of the Holy Spirit on 'all' flesh will be seen **in our day**!!! God will make Himself known to everyone, from the least to the greatest **in our day**!!! By God's grace and the Holy Ghost's power, we will be able to spread the gospel and invite everyone to be a part of God's family **in our day**!!! And people from different backgrounds and ethnicities and beliefs will be drawn together by the light and love and truth of God, and as we move closer to Him, we will be drawn closer together until we meet at the

Hub, Christ Jesus, and we will become One In Him!!! And to that, I say Hallelujah!!! Hallelujah!!! Hallelujah!!! AMEN!!!

The Return to the Original Plan

By the presence and power of the Holy Spirit, we have covered so much ground. We've discussed the beginning of evil in heaven, God's original plan for mankind on earth, the separation nation, why there is this drive within mankind to be divided, the pre-problem solution, and the solution lived out. We discovered a better understanding of the community of believers and reviewed the real Lord's prayer. We asked and then answered two important questions—'Will Jesus' prayer ever be answered?' and 'What's love got to do with it?' We then reviewed the evidence and determined that it is clear that Jesus' prayer has been answered before and will be answered again in our time, and we also confirmed that all are invited—from the least to the greatest—to be a part of this great movement to oneness in Christ Jesus and to be a part of the family of God.

And so now, we prepare to land this plane. We have visited the lofty heights of God's plan for mankind and journeyed over mankind's experience from the fall to our present-day experiences. And having taken in such an expansive view of what has caused division in the experience of man and in Christianity, we will now begin to drop the landing gear, tighten our seat belts, put our seats in their upright position, receive final instructions and prepare to hit the runway by considering the topic, "The Return to the Original."

It was for this reason that Jesus came to earth and restored what had been lost in Eden. His entire ministry was to show mankind the Father, to reveal God's true character, to communicate God's will for mankind, to demonstrate how to live out God's will, to pay the penalty for man's sin, repair the breach, restore the original relationship between man and God, and then return to heaven to serve as our advocate with the Father. And now that Jesus has fulfilled His mission and is sitting at the right hand of the Father interceding for us, it is with confidence that mankind can now believe that, because of what Jesus has done, it is possible to return to the original experience of the God/man relationship, to experience walking and talking and worshiping God like God originally intended.

The reason why we can believe this is because of two prayers that Jesus prayed. We have been focusing on what I have called "the real Lord's Prayer" throughout this book as we have reviewed Jesus' prayer for all believers in John 17:21–23. We have determined that when Jesus prayed for all believers to be one as He and His Father are one, His desire was for us to return to the original God/man relationship and experience. Jesus also communicated His desire for mankind to return to the original God/man relationship and experience when He gave the disciples the model prayer in Matthew 6 and Luke 11. The SDA Commentaries say that the disciples were greatly impressed as they listened to the manner in which Jesus prayed, intimately communing with His heavenly Father as one friend does with another. His praying was different from that of the religious leaders of the day, in fact, from anything else they had heard.

I will add that it was their hearing of this intimate prayer between the Son to His Father that gave the disciples an indication of what it looked like, sounded like and felt like to return to the original, to be in intimate relationship and fellowship with God. So, one of the disciples said to Jesus, "Teach us how to pray like that." It is here that we get our first indication of the first step to returning to the original God/man relationship—prayer. The SDA Commentaries say that formal prayer, expressed in set phrases and seemingly directed to an impersonal God a great way off, lacks the reality and vitality that should distinguish prayer. The disciples thought that if only they could pray as Jesus prayed, their own effectiveness as disciples would be greatly increased.

In view of the fact that Jesus had taught them by precept (Matt. 6:7–15) and example (Luke 9:29) how to pray, it seems likely that upon this occasion, the request came from some disciples who had not been with Jesus upon similar occasions in the past. The term "disciples" need not be confined to the Twelve. These disciples may have been of the Seventy (those that did not have the intimate experience of the Twelve). So, we can see in Luke 11:2–13, the importance that Jesus placed on prayer as a means of returning to the original God/man relationship, for in responding to this request, "Teach us to pray," Jesus took extra time and effort by giving a model prayer, a parable to illustrate the spirit of prayer, and some admonition encouraging faithfulness and diligence in prayer.

In her book, "*Thoughts from the Mount of Blessing*," Ellen White also recognized the importance Jesus placed on this prayer as a means of mankind returning back to the original God/man relationship. She noted that in this model prayer, Jesus wanted the disciples, and all who took on this practice of prayer, to know that God is our Father, who loves and cares for us as His children. He is also the great King of the universe. The interests of His kingdom are our interests, and we are to work for its upbuilding. The disciples of Christ were looking for the immediate coming of the kingdom of His glory, but in giving them this prayer, Jesus taught that the kingdom was not then to be established. They were to pray for its coming as an event yet future. But this petition was also an assurance to them. While they were not to behold the coming of the kingdom in their day, the fact that Jesus bade them pray for it is evidence that in God's own time, it will surely come.

The kingdom of God's grace is now being established, as day by day, hearts that have been full of sin and rebellion yield to the sovereignty of His love. But the full establishment of the kingdom of His glory will not take place until the second coming of Christ to this world. "The kingdom and dominion, and the greatness of the kingdom under the whole heaven, shall be given to the people of the saints of the Most High," (Daniel 7:27 KJV). They shall inherit the kingdom prepared for them "From the foundation of the world," as noted in Matthew 25:34. And Christ will take to Himself His great power and will reign. The heavenly gates are again to be lifted up, and with ten thousand times ten thousand and thousands of thousands of holy ones, our Savior will come forth as King of kings and Lord of lords. Jehovah Immanuel "shall be king over all the earth: in that day shall there be one Lord, and His name one," (Zechariah 14:9 KJV). "The tabernacle of God" shall be with men, "and He will dwell with them, and they shall be His people, and God Himself shall be with them, and be their God," (Revelation 21:3 NKJV).

But before that coming, Jesus said, "This gospel of the kingdom shall be preached in all the world for a witness unto all nations." Matthew 24:14. His kingdom will not come until the good tidings of His grace have been carried to all the earth. Hence, as we give ourselves to God and win other souls to Him, we hasten the coming of His kingdom. Only those who devote themselves to His service, saying, "Here am I; send me" (Isaiah 6:8), to open blind eyes, to turn men "from darkness to light and from the power of Satan unto God, that they may receive forgiveness of sins and inheritance among them which are sanctified," (Acts 26:18), they alone pray in sincerity, "Thy kingdom come."

So, now we see how important it is for us to catch this vision, to recognize the essence of these two prayers, to embrace and join with Jesus in this desire for the kingdom of God to come – both the kingdom of His grace in this present world and His coming kingdom. The SDA Commentaries say that in this life, Christians must make the kingdom supreme in their affections and the great aim of life. That is why we are admonished in Matthew 6:33, "But seek ye first the kingdom of God and His righteousness, and all these things shall be added unto you. "The SDA Commentaries then made it clear that the "kingdom of heaven" was established at the first advent of Christ. Jesus, Himself was King, and those who believed in Him became its subjects. The territory of the kingdom was the hearts and lives of the subjects. Obviously, the message Jesus presented during His ministry referred to the kingdom of divine grace. But, as Jesus Himself made clear, this kingdom of grace was preparatory to the kingdom of glory.

It was here that I realized that the focus on the establishment of the kingdom of glory, which they had mistakenly interpreted to mean a kingdom in which the Romans would be defeated and the Jews would reign as priests and kings, had prevented them from fully understanding the need to establish the kingdom of divine grace. I then realized that some Christians today are making the same mistake as the disciples did. Many Christians are praying for Jesus to come and are looking forward to the kingdom of heaven but have not committed to first participate in the establishment of the kingdom of God's grace, a kingdom that welcomes every sinner to receive the love and grace of God, to receive Jesus as their Savior, to embrace one another in love and be a part of the family of God. This kingdom must come first, and I believe that is why Jesus prayed these two prayers so that we would celebrate the kingdom of grace in preparation to celebrating the kingdom of glory.

And this is really what this book is all about, seeking first the kingdom of God and His righteousness, that kingdom which places the cross of Christ front and center. This kingdom recognizes that the ground is level at the foot of the cross and welcomes all mankind, from the least to the greatest, to come and receive the cleansing from all sin and stain and be recognized as a child of the King. They become citizens of a kingdom in which the light and love and truth of God draws all believers to Him, and as we are drawn closer to Him, we are drawn closer to one another until we become one in Him. And the scripture says, that if we seek first this kingdom and its righteousness, then everything else we desire will be added unto us.

The SDA Commentaries say that there is no such thing as security apart from God and citizenship in His kingdom. That statement emphasizes the point that we must stop trying to find security in jobs, money, possessions, church offices, and positions, even in being a part of a denomination or a particular group. Security can only be found in God and having citizenship in His kingdom, and we mustn't think His kingdom is defined by a denomination, which is man-made. Man-made things are temporary by nature and lead to doubt and worry, and the best cure for worry is to trust in God. If we do our part faithfully, if we make the kingdom of heaven first in our thoughts and lives, God will take care of us on our journey through life. He will graciously "anoint" our heads with oil, and our cup of experience will overflow with good things. This is what our experience will be when we put the kingdom of God first, when we commit to establishing the kingdom of His grace first, which includes committing to being good neighbors in the community of believers, studying and praying and worshiping and praying and studying together, being drawn as a community of believers closer to God and His truth, which will automatically draw us closer to one another. Then one day, if we continue to cooperate with this process, we will return to the original, being a people that at one time were not a people, but now are His own special people that are one in Him.

Let's recognize that in the beginning, there was unity in heaven, and it centered around the worship of God. Several times in scripture, we find heaven portrayed as a unified conglomeration of praise and worship to God. Daniel 7:9–10 speaks of God on His throne with "a thousand thousands" angels ministering to Him and ten thousand times ten thousand standing before Him. Revelation 4:1–11 shows coordinated praise to God with elders and living creatures worshipping Him. It was all about love for and worship of God. On earth, after the Creator had made the perfect place for His prized possession, mankind, His crowning act was to create the Sabbath, a time set aside for showing love for and worship to God and fellowshipping with one another.

Pentecost took place because of the unity among the believers, which centered around studying and fellowshipping, and worshiping God. And in the advent movement, once again, unity among the believers centered around studying and fellowshipping and worshipping of God. I am making this point because I believe, as we consider what has been done in heaven and on earth, that if we want both of Jesus' prayers to be answered, if we want to be a part of facilitating the return to the original God/man relationship, that we must repeat what took place previously. We must seek first to establish the kingdom of God's grace by focusing on loving and studying and fellowshipping and worshiping God as one body of believers. There is only one way for this to happen, and that is to do it Jesus' way, and Jesus' way focuses on oneness. In Matthew 7:13–14 NKJV, Jesus stated: [13] "Enter by the narrow gate; for wide *is* the gate and broad *is* the way that leads to destruction, and there are many who go in by it. [14] [a]Because narrow *is* the gate and [b]difficult *is* the way which leads to life, and there are few who find it." This passage of scripture is just "one" of many Bible passages teaching "oneness." The Bible presents several "oneness" passages:

1. David spoke of one path (Psalm 16:11).

2. Solomon spoke of one path (Proverbs 4:18).

3. Isaiah prophesied of one path (Isaiah 35:8).

4. Jeremiah foretold one way (Jeremiah 32:39).

5. Jesus said there is one way leading unto everlasting life (Matthew 7:13–14).

6. Jesus said, "I am the Way" (John 14:6).

7. Jesus said there is one door (John 10:9).

8. Jesus said there is one Shepherd (John 10:16).

9. Jesus said there is one fold (John 10:16).

10. Jesus built one church (Matthew 16:18).

11. Jesus commissioned the preaching of one Gospel (Mark 16:15–16).

12. Paul knew but one Gospel (Gal. 1:8-9).

13. Ephesians 4:4-6 says, that there is one body, one Spirit, one hope, one Lord, one faith, one baptism, and one God and Father.

14. Matthew 7:28; John 7:16-17; Acts 2:42; Acts 5:28; Romans 6:17; Ephesians 4:14; 1 Timothy 1:3; 2 Timothy 4:2-3 says, that there is but one doctrine.

There is "one" way, not "many" ways; "one" path, not "many" paths; "one" door, not "many" doors; "one" fold, not "many" folds; "one" church, not "many" churches; "one" Gospel, not "many" gospels; "one" doctrine, not "many" doctrines; "one" body, not "many" bodies; "one" Spirit, not "many" spirits; "one" hope, not "many" hopes; "one" Lord, not "many" lords; "one" faith, not "many" faiths; "one" baptism, not "many" baptisms; "one" God and Father, not "many" gods and fathers.

The Bible tells us that there are "many" doctrines of men (Matthew 15:9; Colossians 2:20–22; Hebrews 13:9). There are "many" doctrines of devils (1 Timothy 4:1). In 1 Timothy 4:16, it tells us that a faithful preacher must continue in "the doctrine" of Christ to save himself and those who hear him. When we read 2 John 1:10–11, we learn that we are not to receive into our homes or bid Godspeed to those who bring doctrine other than that of Christ. To do so is to bring "division" into the church of our Lord. What we have been studying in John 17:20–21 tells us that division among the followers of Christ is unscriptural and contrary to Christ's prayer, and Paul's admonition in 1 Corinthians 1:10–13 is "that there be no divisions among you." Let us therefore resolve to adhere to the Bible teaching of "oneness," "that ye stand fast in one spirit, with one mind striving together for the faith of the gospel" (Philippians 1:27) and not to "the commandments of men" (Matthew 15:9; Titus 1:14).

As we close this chapter, can we dream for a minute? Can we, as members of the community of believers, imagine what it would be like for there to be unity among us by being centered on the study and fellowship and worship of the one true and wise God? What would it be like if we truly became one in Him? Imagine the community of believers studying and praying and fellowshipping and worshipping together, surrendering to the Holy Spirit and receiving with joy the truths of God's Word. Imagine that as the community of believers are in dialogue, they not only hear the things that raise concerns but also focus on things that they can agree on, providing a friendly foundation for their conversations. Imagine if their mutual desire to discover the truth together led them not to lord their individual understanding over others but instead share it with humility and love.

Imagine if when the principals of two different and significant theological beliefs are in dialogue, they would consider how their influence and how the dialogue impacts those that are listening, allowing that recognition to govern how they speak. Imagine if, by dialoguing and praying and studying and searching together, all involved would celebrate being drawn closer to God and into unity as a body of believers and not compromise the experience by recruiting for one denomination over another. Imagine...no more separating from one another when our beliefs differ, within or between denominations. Imagine all believers embodying Jesus' prayer in John 17, that we be one as He and His Father are one, so fully, so completely that we would say to each other, "separation is not an option!!!

I believe that it is in doing this that we would cooperate with the process of being drawn to the hub and being drawn closer together. We must trust in the Word of God enough to let it have its perfect work in us. Let's be patient with the process. At times it might seem difficult, maybe contentious and combative, and may even lead us to want to give up and retreat to our denominational safe place, but let's not give up. James

1:2–6KJV says, "My brethren, count it all joy when ye fall into divers temptations; knowing this, that the trying of your faith worketh patience. But let patience have her perfect work, that ye may be perfect and entire, wanting nothing. If any of you lack wisdom, let him ask of God, that giveth to all men liberally, and upbraideth not; and it shall be given him. But let him ask in faith, nothing wavering. For he that wavereth is like a wave of the sea driven with the wind and tossed.

And yes, y'all, this may be the time to shed some labels/traditions/mindsets, but at the end of the day, as we all journey toward that Jeremiah 29:11 "expected end/future and hope," my prayer is that we as children of God and followers of Christ will have conducted His business in a way that leads to His John 17:21–23 prayer being answered—that we will become one in Him, that our actions will allow His glory to be received by and seen in us, that we will be led to return to the original God/man relationship, that His kingdom of grace will come, so that the world will know the truth about Him by seeing the truth in and hearing the truth from us. And when THIS gospel of the kingdom has been preached in all the world, then Jesus will come, and we can truly return to the original, to what God has always wanted—for His children, from the least to the greatest, to be with Him in glory. Hallelujah!!!

A Glorious Ending!!!

S o, as we end this incredible journey, the Holy Spirit has clearly shown us the many facets of what Jesus had in mind when He prayed that prayer in John 17 for all believers. We have come to the realization that it was not just an empty wish or a wistful suggestion. Jesus truly did and still does want all believers in Him to be one. And after reviewing all the angles, God's original plan for unity, the war against unity in heaven, the fall from unity in the Garden, mankind's challenges with unity down through the years, and the culminating events that will restore unity in the last days, I pray that we all have come to the conclusion that God will have His way. We must believe that what was once lost will be restored, and that we as His last-day children want to be a part of Jesus' prayer being answered in our lives and in the lives of all His special people. And as our wheels hit the runway and we taxi this plane to a stop, as we reflect on the journey and all that we discussed, some topics which may have seemed somewhat turbulent may have challenged our thinking and made the ride a little bumpy for our denominational seating. However, I want to leave you all, as faithful passengers who weathered the entire journey, with a word of gratitude for staying until the end. And as this journey concludes, I want to give you a few of the marvelous highlights of the wonderful place in which we have landed, that expected glorious ending.

We ended the previous chapter dreaming, imagining what a united community of believers would look like. And as we unbuckle our seatbelts and stand to stretch after this extended journey, I would like for us to consider the special seat we have been given as believers. I know I have spent the majority of this study talking about the wagon wheel concept, how the many spokes represent all believers who are making their way to the Hub, which represents Jesus, and how we must not spend time trying to get people to jump from their spoke to our spoke, but how instead we should be fostering the movement of everyone towards Jesus. We discussed how all believers should move toward Jesus on their present denominational spoke, how as we draw closer to Him, the gap, the separation, the division between us would grow smaller and smaller, and we will draw closer and closer to one another until we meet at the Hub and will be one in Christ Jesus.

For some, it may have seemed that I was diminishing the importance of their particular beliefs. However, I believe that I was led to present this topic this way because, without a doubt, there is a prophetic magnificence to all that we together bring to the table. As a Seventh-day Adventist Christian, and using the advent movement that marked the beginning of this denomination as an example, one could see that the message

God revealed to that small, multi-denominational group in 1844 was a pivotal revelation from God to prepare mankind for the culmination of His great plan of salvation and the coming of Jesus. The advent message identified during that experience was of significant importance for the whole world.

However, any teacher or coach who realizes that a particular group of children has been gifted and possess something special, that has an ability or a knowledge, or an understanding that sets them apart from the other children must also help them manage their giftedness. It may require that their attention be directed away from their giftedness just so they can first recognize and understand that even though they are special, their being a part of the community is what matters most. I believe that this is the case with Adventists and other denominations. If too much time is spent focusing on and highlighting how special they are because of their 'truth,' how their message makes them special and how they must take 'their' message to the world, it will foster a sentiment that I believe has plagued the body of Christ for many years.

If this study had been done in a way that elevated any one denomination, some of us would have come away continuing to think that we are better than other believers that may be traveling on other spokes of the wagon wheel. But as we survey the landscape at the end of this journey to this place of oneness in Christ Jesus, I would like to take a few minutes for us to recognize the part we each play in making this place of oneness and the ending God has in mind for all believers, so glorious.

The advent message given to that small group of believers was intended to be the unifying message that brought God's people from various denominations together under the banner of His truth. The revelations that were given, especially the understanding of the Three Angel's Messages, were intended by God to prepare a people for the coming of the Lord. Ellen White, who was a leader in the formation of the Seventh-day Adventist Church and displayed the prophetic gift, called the advent message a gathering message, one in which those that heard and responded to God's truth would be gathered together in unity under that truth. Read these quotes by Ellen White from Adventist Review and Sabbath Herald (ARSH):

❖ Thank the Lord. Who will not enjoy this blessed Millennium? All its blessings, its glory, and its joy are for all. And in the Third Angel's Message, the preparatory, gathering call of this grand Millennium is now sounding to every nation and kindred and tongue and people. Listen to the call. Accept the invitation. Get ready, get ready, get ready. ARSH January 30, 1900, page 73.2

❖ Yes, it is our privilege to live so that we may receive a copious shower. Covet earnestly the best gifts. 1 Corinthians 12:31. The proclamation of the third angel's message is gathering out a people and purifying them by its searching and solemn truths, so that God can safely bestow or impart all the gifts and graces once enjoyed when the Holy Spirit came down like a rushing mighty wind in the former rain. ARSH July 10, 1860, page 61.4

❖ But how unworthy to speak or write in his name. My soul is bowed with reverence as I write, his mercy has been so great in giving me to see and keep the true Sabbath, and to see all his past wonderful work in the advent movement, and now the third angel's message, which is gathering the remnant into the "unity of the faith" and the knowledge of the Son of God. O, I do want to take to myself the whole armor, that I may have a shield from the power of Satan, and be kept from the hour of temptation, that is soon coming upon all the world, and stand at last upon the sea of glass with the 144,000. Blessed release! Cheer up, ye weary ones; remember, some crowns will have many stars. I long to have those who have borne the burden and heat of the day receive them. ARSH November 25, 1851, page 56.1

Oh, my fellow believers, I hope we can see what God intended by providing experiences such as the advent message and what our witness should be as a result. God's revelations to His people were not given to them to lay claim on it as theirs and to dole it out as if it is under their control. What God intended was for them to take this message to the world so that believers in the Lord Jesus Christ would receive these beautiful truths and become united under the banner of Christ Jesus. It is when we commit to this cause, that the latter rain will fall, giving us 'dunamis,' dynamite power to preach this message in a way that will draw those who are of other folds into the one-fold of the Good Shephard. And this fold does not have a particular denominational name above it. It is called the kingdom of God's grace, which is preparing a people for the kingdom of glory.

And this is where this plane has landed, in a place where all believers understand and receive the reality of being one in Christ Jesus, where they all will be recognized by heaven as citizens of the kingdom. It is this citizenship that will prepare God's special people for the final leg of the journey to the kingdom of glory.

As I close with this view of our glorious ending, I want to take us to one of my favorite scenes of heaven found in Revelation 7:9–15 NKJV. The scripture says, ⁹ "After these things I looked, and behold, a great multitude which no one could number, of all nations, tribes, peoples, and tongues" (people of all different backgrounds and denominations and...), "standing before the throne and before the Lamb, clothed with white robes, with palm branches in their hands, ¹⁰ and crying out with a loud voice, saying, 'Salvation belongs to our God who sits on the throne, and to the Lamb!'" ¹¹ All the angels stood around the throne and the elders and the four living creatures, and fell on their faces before the throne and worshiped God, ¹² saying: "Amen! Blessing and glory and wisdom, Thanksgiving and honor and power and might, Be to our God forever and ever. Amen." ¹³ Then one of the elders answered, saying to me, "Who are these arrayed in white robes, and where did they come from?" ¹⁴ And I said to him, "Sir, you know." So, he said to me, "These are the ones who come out of the great tribulation, and washed their robes and made them white in the blood of the Lamb. [15] Therefore they are before the throne of God and serve Him day and night in His temple. And He who sits on the throne will dwell among them."

My brothers and sisters, this is the glorious ending God has in store for the body of Christ, the community of believers, and His own special people. As that gospel wheel keeps turning, believers on each spoke keep moving closer and closer to Jesus and closer and closer to one another. Not everybody is going to get on that wheel. All won't accept this last-day message. But that is not our business. All we are to do is lift up the banner of Christ and let the light and love of God's truth have its way. And for all who respond and continue their journey toward Jesus, that gap between His people will grow smaller and smaller until one day we will all meet at the Hub, Christ Jesus. And when Jesus comes to gather His children, this may be what Ezekiel saw, a wheel in a wheel, way in the middle of the air. I don't know for sure, but I believe there's going to be a Holy Ghost party at the hub of that wagon wheel, and as that wheel makes its way to glory, we all will celebrate until we land on the peaceful shore, and we will stand before our God, and cast our crowns at His feet, and sing that song that the angels can't sing. Oh, my brothers and sisters, let us make sure that we stand in unity here on earth so that Jesus' prayer will have been answered, and we will be one in Him and stand in unity before the throne of God. AMEN, AMEN, AND AMEN!!!

ABOUT THE AUTHOR

Mark A Brown holds a B. A in Information Systems Management and is a Biblical Entrepreneurship certified trainer and Coach. In addition, he founded an inmate re-entry preparation program, is the chapter President of Mid-Atlantic ministry, serves on the executive board of a non-profit, and functions as Power of Attorney for senior citizens.

Born of humble beginnings, Mark retired from a 37-year federal career and has remained fully engaged in life by starting his own business, traveling to Kenya to serve, and volunteering in the local correctional facility. When possible, he engages his love for music by making an effort to maintain his

50+ year relationship with the trombone and his beginner status with the guitar.

He loves spending time with his family, working outdoors, helping his wife with her garden, and taking walks. Mark A Brown is a father and grandfather who resides in Montgomery Village, MD, with his wife, Karen.

To learn more about this movement and to connect with Mark visit www.1inhim.com

or email mark@1inhim.com